FREMDSPRACHENTEXTE

T. C. Boyle

After the Plague and Other Stories

Herausgegeben von
Sylvia Mayer und Graham Wilson

Philipp Reclam jun. Stuttgart

Diese Ausgabe darf nur in der Bundesrepublik Deutschland, in Österreich und in der Schweiz vertrieben werden.

RECLAMS UNIVERSAL-BIBLIOTHEK Nr. 9149

Gesamtherstellung: Reclam, Ditzingen. Printed in Germany 2006
RECLAM, UNIVERSAL-BIBLIOTHEK und RECLAMS
UNIVERSAL-BIBLIOTHEK sind eingetragene Marken
der Philipp Reclam jun. GmbH & Co., Stuttgart
ISBN-13: 978-3-15-009149-4
ISBN-10: 3-15-009149-7

www.reclam.de

Heart of a Champion

We scan the cornfields and the wheatfields winking gold and goldbrown and yellowbrown in the midday sun, on up the grassy slope to the barn redder than red against the sky bluer than blue, across the smooth stretch of the barnyard with its pecking chickens, and then right on up to the screen door at the back of the house. The door swings open, a black hole in the sun, and Timmy emerges with his corn-silk hair, corn-fed face. He is dressed in crisp overalls, striped T-shirt, stubby blue Keds. There'd have to be a breeze – and we're not disappointed – his clean fine cup-cut hair waves and settles as he scuffs across the barnyard and out to the edge of the field. The boy stops there to gaze out over the nodding wheat, eyes unsquinted

2 **to wink:** funkeln.
4 **barn:** Schuppen, Stall.
6 **to peck:** picken.
7 **screen door:** Tür mit Fliegengitter.
10 **crisp:** frisch, adrett.
11 **stubby:** dick.
Keds: Turnschuh-Marke (seit 1916).
12 **cup-cut:** Topfschnitt.
13 **to scuff:** schlurfen.
15 **to gaze:** blicken.
to nod: nicken, wogen.
unsquinted: ohne zu blinzeln.

despite the sun, and blue as tinted lenses. Then he brings three fingers to his lips in a neat triangle and whistles long and low, sloping up sharp to cut off at the peak. A moment passes: he whistles again. And then we see it – way out there at the far corner of the field – the ripple, the dashing furrow, the blur of the streaking dog, white chest, flashing feet.

They're in the woods now. The boy whistling, hands in pockets, kicking along with his short baby-fat strides; the dog beside him wagging the white tip of her tail like an all-clear flag. They pass beneath an arching old black-barked oak. It creaks. And suddenly begins to fling itself down on them: immense, brutal: a panzer strike. The boy's eyes startle and then there's a blur, a smart snout clutching his

1 **tinted:** gefärbt.
2 **triangle:** Dreieck.
3 **sloping up sharp:** abrupt ansteigend.
4 **peak:** höchster Punkt.
6 **ripple:** sanftes Wogen.
dashing furrow: rasch entstehende Furche.
blur: verschwommene Gestalt.
7 **to streak:** flitzen.
10 **stride:** Schritt, Gang.
to wag: (mit etwas) wedeln, (etwas) hin und her bewegen.
11 **all-clear flag:** Entwarnungsfahne.
12 **to arch:** sich biegen.
to creak: knarren.
13 **to fling o.s. down:** sich auf den Boden werfen, zu Boden stürzen.
14 **to startle:** erschrecken.
15 **snout:** Schnauze.
to clutch s.th.: etwas packen, umklammert halten.

pantleg, the thunderblast of the trunk, the dust and spinning leaves. "Golly, Lassie … I didn't even see it," says the boy sitting safe in a mound of moss. The collie looks up at him (the svelte snout, the deep gold logician's eyes), and laps at his face.

And now they're down by the river. The water is brown with angry suppurations, spiked with branches, fence posts, tires and logs. It rushes like the sides of boxcars – and chews deep and insidious at the bank under Timmy's feet. The roar is like a jetport: little wonder he can't hear the dog's warning bark. We watch the crack appear, widen to a ditch; then the halves separating (snatch of red earth, writhe of worm), the poise and pitch, and Timmy crushing down with it. Just a flash – but already he's way downstream, his head like a plastic jug, dashed and bobbed, spinning toward the nasty mouth of the falls.

1 **thunderblast:** donnernder Aufprall.
2 **golly** (coll.): Menschenskind!
Lassie: Name des vielleicht bekanntesten Collie überhaupt; Fernsehserie in den USA von 1958 bis 1974 (581 Folgen); auch 7 Spielfilme.
3 **mound:** Hügel.
4 **svelte:** grazil.
5 **to lap at s.th.:** etwas belecken.
7 **suppurations:** Vereiterungen; (fig.) Eiterbeulen.
9 **boxcar:** Güterwagen.
insidious: heimtückisch.
10 **jetport:** Flugplatz für Düsenflugzeuge.
12 **ditch:** Graben.
13 **snatch:** Stück, Brocken.
13f. **writhe of worm:** sich drehende und windende Würmer.
14 **poise and pitch:** Schweben und Hinunterstürzen.
17 **to bob:** sich auf und ab bewegen.
mouth of the falls (pl.): Schlund des Wasserfalls.

But there's the dog – fast as a struck match – bursting along the bank all white and gold melded in motion, hair sleeked with the wind of it, legs beating time to the panting score. … Yet what can she hope to do? – the current surges on, lengths ahead, sure bet to win the race to the falls. Timmy sweeps closer, sweeps closer, the falls loud now as a hundred tympani, the war drums of the Sioux, Africa gone bloodlust mad! The dog strains, lashing over the wet earth like a whipcrack; strains every last ganglion and dendrite until finally she draws abreast of him. Then she's in the air, the foaming yellow water. Her paws churning like pistons, whiskers chuffing with the exertion – oh the roar! – and there, she's got him, her sure jaws clamping down on the shirt collar, her eyes fixed on the slip of rock at the falls' edge. Our blood races, organs palpitate. The black brink of the falls, the white

2 **melded:** verschmolzen.
3 **sleeked:** geglättet.
4 **to pant:** hecheln.
5 **to surge:** vorpreschen.
7 **tympani:** Timpani, Kesselpauken.
8 **Sioux:** Gruppe von nordamerikanischen Indianervölkern in den Bundesstaaten Minnesota sowie North und South Dakota.
9 **to lash:** peitschen, sausen.
10 **ganglion:** Ganglion, Nervenknoten.
dendrite: Dendrit, Fortsatz einer Nervenzelle.
11 **to draw abreast of s.o.:** auf gleiche Höhe mit jdm. kommen.
12 **paw:** Pfote.
12f. **to churn like pistons:** wie Kolben wirbeln.
13 **whiskers:** Barthaare, Bart.
to chuff with exertion: vor Anstrengung puffen, zittern.
17 **to palpitate:** zittern, heftig klopfen.
brink: Rand.

paws digging at the rock – and then they're safe. The collie sniffs at Timmy's inert little form, nudges his side until she manages to roll him over. Then clears his tongue and begins mouth-to-mouth.

Night: the barnyard still, a bulb burning over the screen door. Inside, the family sit at dinner, the table heaped with pork chops, mashed potatoes, applesauce and peas, a pitcher of clean white milk. Home-baked bread. Mom and Dad, their faces sexless, bland, perpetually good-humored and sympathetic, poise stiff-backed, forks in midswoop, while Timmy tells his story: "So then Lassie grabbed me by the collar and golly I musta blanked out cause I don't remember anything more till I woke up on the rock –"

"Well I'll be," says Mom.

"You're lucky you've got such a good dog, son," says Dad, gazing down at the collie where she lies patiently, snout over paw, tail wapping the floor. She is combed and washed and fluffed, her lashes mascaraed

2 **inert:** unbeweglich.
to nudge: anstupsen.
7 **mashed potatoes** (pl.): Kartoffelpüree.
8 **pitcher:** Krug.
9 **bland:** leer, farblos.
11 **forks in midswoop:** mit angehobenen Gabeln.
13 **musta** (coll.): *must have.*
to blank out (coll.): ohnmächtig werden.
15 **I'll be** (coll.): Ich glaub, mich laust der Affe!
18 **to wap s.th.:** gegen, auf etwas schlagen.
19 **fluffed:** flauschig.
lashes: Wimpern.

and curled, her chest and paws white as dishsoap. She looks up humbly. But then her ears leap, her neck jerks round – and she's up at the door, head cocked, alert. A high yipping yowl like a stuttering fire whistle shudders through the room. And then another. The dog whines.

"Darn," says Dad. "I thought we were rid of those coyotes – next thing they'll be after the chickens again."

The moon blanches the yard, leans black shadows on the trees, the barn. Upstairs in the house, Timmy lies sleeping in the pale light, his hair fastidiously mussed, his breathing gentle. The collie lies on the throw rug beside the bed. We see that her eyes are open. Suddenly she rises and slips to the window, silent as a shadow. And looks down the long elegant snout to the barnyard below, where the coyote slinks from shade to shade, a limp pullet dangling from his

1 **dishsoap:** Kernseife.
3 **to cock one's head:** den Kopf in die Höhe heben.
4 **alert:** wachsam.
to yip: kläffen.
yowl: Jaulen, Heulen.
6 **to whine:** jaulen.
7 **darn** (coll.): verflixt!, verdammt!
10 **to blanch:** bleich machen, in bleiches Licht tauchen.
12 f. **fastidiously mussed:** gewollt unordentlich (*to muss* [coll.]: verstrubbeln).
14 **throw rug:** kleiner Teppich.
17 **to slink:** schleichen.
18 **limp:** schlaff, leblos.
pullet: junges Huhn.
to dangle: baumeln, herabhängen.

jaws. He is stunted, scabious, syphilitic, his forepaw trap-twisted, his eyes running. The collie whimpers softly from behind the window. And the coyote stops in mid-trot, frozen in a cold shard of light, ears high on his head. Then drops the chicken at his feet, leers up at the window and begins a soft, crooning, sad-faced song.

The screen door slaps behind Timmy as he bolts from the house, Lassie at his heels. Mom's head emerges on the rebound. "Timmy!" (He stops as if jerked by a rope, turns to face her.) "You be home before lunch, hear?"

"Sure, Mom," he says, already spinning off, the dog by his side. We get a close-up of Mom's face: she is smiling a benevolent boys-will-be-boys smile. Her teeth are perfect.

In the woods Timmy steps on a rattler and the dog bites its head off. "Gosh," he says. "Good girl, Las-

1 **stunted:** verkümmert.
scabious: räudig.
syphilitic: syphilitisch.
2 **to whimper:** winseln.
4 **shard:** Scherbe, Splitter.
5 **to leer:** anzüglich grinsen.
6 **to croon:** schmachtend singen, balzen.
8 **to slap:** zuschlagen, -fallen.
to bolt: (davon)stürmen.
10 **on the rebound:** gleich darauf.
14 **close-up:** Großaufnahme.
15 **benevolent:** wohlwollend, nachsichtig.
17 **rattler:** *rattlesnake:* Klapperschlange.
18 **gosh:** Mensch!, Mann!

sie." Then he stumbles and slips over an embankment, rolls down the brushy incline and over a sudden precipice, whirling out into the breathtaking blue space like a sky diver. He thumps down on a narrow ledge twenty feet below. And immediately scrambles to his feet, peering timorously down the sheer wall to the heap of bleached bone at its base. Small stones break loose, shoot out like asteroids. Dirt-slides begin. But Lassie yarps reassuringly from above, sprints back to the barn for a winch and cable, hoists the boy to safety.

On their way back for lunch Timmy leads them through a still and leaf-darkened copse. We remark how odd it is that the birds and crickets have left off their cheeping, how puzzling that the background

1 f. **embankment:** Böschung.
2 **incline:** Hang.
3 **precipice:** Abgrund.
to whirl: wirbeln.
4 **sky diver:** Fallschirmspringer.
to thump: plumpsen.
5 **ledge:** (schmaler Fels-)Vorsprung.
6 **to peer:** schielen, spähen.
timorously (adv.): ängstlich.
7 **sheer:** steil, jäh.
bleached: (von der Sonne) gebleicht.
8 **asteroid:** Asteroid, kleiner Planet.
9 **to yarp:** kläffen.
reassuringly (adv.): beruhigend.
10 **winch:** Winde.
11 **to hoist:** hieven, hochziehen.
13 **copse:** Wäldchen.
14 **cricket:** Grille.
15 **cheeping:** Gepiepse, Zirpen.

music has begun to rumble so. Suddenly, round a bend in the path before them, the coyote appears. Nose to the ground, intent, unaware of them. But all at once he jerks to a halt, shudders like an epileptic, the hackles rising, tail dipping between his legs. The collie too stops short, just yards away, her chest proud and shaggy and white. The coyote cowers, bunches like a cat, glares at them. Timmy's face sags with alarm. The coyote lifts his lip. But then, instead of leaping at her adversary's throat, the collie prances up and stretches her nose out to him, her eyes soft as a leading lady's, round as a doe's. She's balsamed and perfumed; her full chest tapers a lovely S to her sleek haunches and sculpted legs. He is puny, runted, half her size, his coat like a discarded doormat. She circles

1 **to rumble:** dröhnen, grollen.
5 **hackles** (pl.): Nackenfell.
7 **shaggy:** zottelig.
to cower: kauern, sich ducken.
to bunch: hier: einen Buckel machen.
8 **to glare at s.o.:** jdn. anstarren.
to sag: zusammensacken, in sich zusammenfallen.
10 **adversary:** Gegner, Feind.
10f. **to prance up:** herbeitänzeln.
12 **leading lady:** Hauptdarstellerin.
doe: Reh, Ricke.
balsamed: mit Balsam parfümiert.
13 **to taper:** spitz zulaufen.
sleek: geschmeidig, glatt.
14 **haunches:** Hinterbeine.
sculpted: (wie) gemeißelt, wohlgeformt.
puny: mickrig.
runted: untersetzt.
15 **discarded:** weggeworfen.

him now, sniffing. She whimpers, he growls: throaty and tough, the bad guy. And stands stiff while she licks at his whiskers, noses at his rear, the bald black scrotum. Timmy is horror-struck. Then, the music sweeping off in birdtrills of flute and harpstring, the coyote slips round behind, throat thrown back, black lips tight with anticipation.

"What was she doing, Dad?" Timmy asks over his milk and sandwich.

"The sky was blue today, son," he says.

"But she had him trapped, Dad – they were stuck together end to end and I thought we had that wicked old coyote but then she went and let him go – what's got into her, Dad?"

"The barn was red today, son," he says.

Late afternoon: the sun mellow, more orange than white. Purpling clots of shadow hang from the branches, ravel out from the tree trunks. Bees and wasps and flies saw away at the wet full-bellied air. Timmy and the dog are far out beyond the north

1 **to growl:** knurren.
4 **scrotum:** Hodensack.
5 **harpstring:** Harfensaite(n); Harfenklang.
7 **anticipation:** Erwartung, Vorfreude.
16 **mellow:** mild.
17 **to purple:** dunkelrot werden; sich violett verfärben.
clot: Klumpen.
18 **to ravel out:** ausfransen.
19 **to saw away** (coll.): (auf einem Instrument) drauflossägen.
full-bellied: (fig.) gesättigt.

pasture, out by the old Indian burial mound, where the boy stoops now to search for arrowheads. Oddly, the collie is not watching him: instead she's pacing the crest above, whimpering softly, pausing from time to time to stare out across the forest, her eyes distant and moonstruck. Behind her, storm clouds squat on the horizon like dark kidneys or brains.

We observe the wind kicking up: leaves flapping like wash, saplings quivering, weeds whipping. It darkens quickly now, the clouds scudding low and smoky over the treetops, blotting the sun from view. Lassie's white is whiter than ever, high-lighted against the dark horizon, the wind-whipped hair foaming around her. Still she doesn't look down at the boy: he digs, dirty-kneed, stoop-backed, oblivious. Then the first fat random drops, a flash, the volcanic blast of thunder. Timmy glances over his shoulder at the noise: he's just in time to watch the scorched pine

1 **pasture:** Weide(land).
burial mound: Grabhügel.
2 **arrowhead:** Pfeilspitze.
4 **crest:** (Hügel-)Kamm.
6 **moonstruck:** mondsüchtig.
to squat: hocken.
8 **to flap:** flattern.
9 **wash: 1.** (zum Trocknen aufgehängte) Wäsche; **2.** Wellengang.
sapling: junger Baum.
to quiver: beben.
10 **to scud:** flitzen, jagen.
11 **to blot:** verdecken, verbergen.
15 **oblivious:** weltvergessen, nicht bewusst.
16 **random:** vereinzelt.
18 **scorched:** versengt.

plummeting toward the constellated freckles in the center of his forehead. Now the collie turns – too late! – the *swoosh-whack!* of the tree, the trembling needles. She's there in an instant, tearing at the green welter, struggling through to his side. He lies unconscious in the muddying earth, hair artistically arranged, a thin scratch painted on his cheek. The trunk lies across the small of his back like the tail of a brontosaurus. The rain falls.

Lassie tugs doggedly at a knob in the trunk, her pretty paws slipping in the wet – but it's no use – it would take a block and tackle, a crane, an army of Bunyans to shift that stubborn bulk. She falters, licks at his ear, whimpers. We observe the troubled look in her eye as she hesitates, uncertain, priorities warring: should she stand guard, or dash for help? The decision is sure and swift – her eyes firm with purpose and she's off like a shard of shrapnel, already up the hill, shooting past the dripping trees, over the river, already cleaving through the high wet banks of wheat.

1 **to plummet:** (hinab)stürzen.
constellated freckles: (zusammen)gruppierte Sommersprossen.
4f. **green welter:** grüne Masse von Nadeln und Ästen.
8 **small of the back:** Kreuz.
10 **to tug at s.th.:** an etwas zerren, ziehen.
doggedly (adv.): hartnäckig, beharrlich.
knob: Verdickung, Knoten.
12 **block and tackle:** Kloben und Hebezeug.
12f. **army of Bunyans:** Armee von Riesenholzfällern (*Paul Bunyan:* fiktiver amerikanischer Riesenholzfäller; Symbol für Kraft).
13 **to falter:** zögern.
18 **shard of shrapnel:** Granatsplitter.
20 **to cleave:** sich den Weg bahnen.

A moment later she's dashing through the puddled and rain-screened barnyard, barking right on up to the back door, where she pauses to scratch daintily, her voice high-pitched and insistent. Mom swings open the door and the collie pads in, claws clacking on the shiny linoleum. "What is it girl? What's the matter? Where's Timmy?"

"Yarf! Yarfata-yarf-yarf!"

"O my! Dad! Dad, come quickly!"

Dad rushes in, his face stolid and reassuring as the Lincoln Memorial. "What is it, dear? … Why, Lassie?"

"Oh Dad, Timmy's trapped under a pine tree out by the old Indian burial ground –"

"Arpit-arp."

"– a mile and a half past the north pasture."

Dad is quick, firm, decisive. "Lassie – you get back up there and stand watch over Timmy … Mom and I'll go for Doc Walker. Hurry now!"

The collie hesitates at the door: "Rarf-arrar-ra!"

"Right," says Dad. "Mom, fetch the chain saw."

1 **puddled:** mit Pfützen übersät.
3 **daintily** (adv.): zierlich, anmutig.
4 **insistent:** aufdringlich, nachdrücklich.
5 **to pad:** trotten.
claw: Kralle.
10 **stolid:** beharrlich, ruhig.
11 **Lincoln Memorial:** große Statue in Washington; errichtet 1915–22 als Monument für Abraham Lincoln (1809–65), Präsident der USA 1861–65.
21 **chain saw:** Kettensäge.

We're back in the woods now. A shot of the mud-running burial mound locates us – yes, there's the fallen pine, and there: Timmy. He lies in a puddle, eyes closed, breathing slow. The hiss of the rain is loud as static. We see it at work: scattering leaves, digging trenches, inciting streams to swallow their banks. It lies deep now in the low areas, and in the mid areas, and in the high areas. Then a shot of the dam, some indeterminate (but short we presume) distance off, the yellow water churning over its lip like urine, the ugly earthen belly distended, blistered with the pressure. Raindrops pock the surface like a plague.

Suddenly the music plunges to those thunderous crouching chords – we're back at the pine now – what is it? There: the coyote. Sniffing, furtive, the malicious eyes, the crouch and slink. He stiffens when he spots

1 **shot:** (Film-)Aufnahme, Bild.
2 **to locate s.o.:** jdn. platzieren, jdm. den Ort angeben.
4 **hiss:** Zischen.
5 **static:** (durch Elektrizität verursachte) atmosphärische Störungen.
6 **trench:** Graben.
to incite: aufhetzen, aufwiegeln, veranlassen.
9 **indeterminate:** unbestimmt.
11 **distended:** aufgebläht.
blistered: voller Blasen, Beulen.
12 **to pock:** mit Pusteln, Pocken übersäen; durchlöchern.
plague: Pest, Seuche.
13 **to plunge:** stürmen, stürzen, preschen.
14 **crouching:** hier etwa: lauernd.
chord: Akkord.
15 **furtive:** verstohlen.
malicious: boshaft.
16 **crouch and slink:** Kauern und Schleichen, geduckte und verstohlene Bewegungen.

the boy – but then slouches closer, a rubbery dangle drooling from between his mismeshed teeth. Closer. Right over the prone figure now, those ominous chords setting up ominous vibrations in our bowels. He stoops, head dipping between his shoulders, irises caught in the corners of his eyes: wary, sly, predatory: the vulture slavering over the fallen fawn.

But wait! – here comes the collie, sprinting out of the wheatfield, bounding rock to rock across the crazed river, her limbs contourless with sheer speed and purpose, the music racing in a mad heroic prestissimo!

The jolting front seat of a Ford. Dad, Mom and the Doctor, all dressed in rain slickers and flap-brimmed rain hats, sitting shoulder to shoulder behind the clap-

---

1 **to slouch closer:** sich geduckt nähern.
rubbery dangle: herabhängendes gummiartiges Gebilde.
2 **to drool:** sabbern.
mismeshed: schlecht ineinander greifend, schief gestellt.
3 **prone:** auf dem Bauch liegend.
ominous: unheilvoll, düster.
4 **bowels:** Eingeweide.
6 **wary:** vorsichtig, wachsam.
sly: schlau, listig.
predatory: raubtierhaft.
7 **vulture:** Geier.
to slaver: sabbern, geifern.
fawn: Rehkitz.
10 **crazed:** verrückt spielend.
13 **to jolt:** rütteln.
14 **rain slicker:** Regenjacke.
flap-brimmed: mit klappbarem Rand.

ping wipers. Their jaws set with determination, eyes aflicker with pioneer gumption.

The coyote's jaws, serrated grinders, work at the tough bone and cartilage of Timmy's left hand. The boy's eyelids flutter with the pain, and he lifts his head feebly – but almost immediately it slaps down again, flat and volitionless, in the mud. At that instant Lassie blazes over the hill like a cavalry charge, show-dog indignation aflame in her eyes. The scrag of a coyote looks up at her, drooling blood, choking down frantic bits of flesh. Looks up at her from eyes that go back thirty million years, savage and bloodlustful and free. Looks up unmoved, uncringing, the bloody snout and steady yellow eyes less a physical challenge than philosophical. We watch the collie's expression alter in midbound – the look of offended AKC morality giving way, dissolving. She skids to a halt, drops

2 **aflicker:** flackernd, glühend.
gumption (coll.): Erfindungsgabe, Grips.
3 **serrated grinders:** gezackte Mahlzähne.
4 **cartilage:** Knorpel.
7 **volitionless:** willenlos.
8 **to blaze:** schießen, sausen.
9 **indignation:** Entrüstung.
scrag: mageres Tier, ‚Gerippe'.
10 **to choke down:** herunterwürgen.
13 **uncringing:** ohne zurückzuschrecken.
16 **in midbound:** mitten im Sprung.
AKC: Abk. für *The American Kennel Club:* exklusiver Hundeverein in den USA.
17 **to dissolve:** verschwinden.
to skid to a halt: schlitternd zum Stehen kommen.

her tail and approaches him, a buttery gaze in her golden eyes. She licks the blood from his lips.

The dam. Impossibly swollen, rain festering the yellow surface, a hundred new streams a minute rampaging in, the pressure of those millions of gallons hard-punching those millions more. There! the first gap, the water spewing out, a burst bubo. And now the dam shudders, splinters, falls to pieces like so much cheap pottery. The roar is devastating.

The two animals start at that terrible rumbling, and still working their gummy jaws, they dash up the far side of the hill. We watch the white-tipped tail retreating side by side with the hacked and tick-blistered gray one – wagging like raggled banners as they disappear into the trees at the top of the rise. We're left with a tableau: the rain, the fallen pine in the crotch of

1 **buttery:** schmeichlerisch.
gaze: Blick.
3 **to fester:** (fig.) schwären lassen.
4 f. **to rampage:** toben, wüten.
7 **to spew out:** sich ergießen.
burst bubo: aufgeplatzte Eiterbeule.
8 **to splinter:** zerbersten.
9 **pottery:** Töpferware.
devastating: verheerend, niederschmetternd.
11 **gummy:** mit viel Zahnfleisch.
13 **hacked:** verstümmelt.
tick-blistered: voller Zecken.
14 **raggled:** zerlumpt.
16 **tableau:** wirkungsvoll gruppiertes Bild.
crotch: Boden.

the valley's V, the spot of the boy's head. And that chilling roar in our ears. Suddenly the wall of water appears at the far end of the V, smashing through the little declivity like a god-sized fist, prickling with shattered trunks and boulders, grinding along like a quick-melted glacier, like planets in collision. We cut to Timmy: eyes closed, hair plastered, his left arm looking as though it should be wrapped in butcher's paper. How? we wonder. How will they ever get him out of this? But then we see them – Mom, Dad and the Doctor – struggling up that same rise, rushing with the frenetic music now, the torrent seething closer, booming and howling. Dad launches himself in full charge down the hillside – but the water is already sweeping over the fallen pine, lifting it like paper – there's a blur, a quick clip of a typhoon at sea (is that a flash of blond hair?), and it's over. The valley is filled to the top of the rise, the water ribbed and rushing like the

2 **to chill:** das Blut in den Adern gefrieren, erstarren lassen.
4 **declivity:** Abhang.
to prickle: stechen.
4f. **shattered:** geborsten.
5 **boulder:** Felsbrocken.
6 **glacier:** Gletscher.
7 **plastered:** angekleistert, verklebt.
12 **frenetic:** hektisch, wild.
torrent: Sturzbach.
to seethe: schäumen, sieden.
12f. **to boom:** dröhnen.
13 **to launch o.s.:** sich stürzen.
14 **to sweep:** rauschen.
16 **typhoon:** Taifun, Wirbelsturm.
18 **ribbed:** gerippt.

Colorado in adolescence. Dad's pants are wet to the crotch.

Mom's face, the Doctor's. Rain. And then the opening strains of the theme song, one violin at first, swelling in mournful mid-American triumph as the full orchestra comes in, tearful, beautiful, heroic, sweeping us up and out of the dismal rain, back to the golden wheatfields in the midday sun. The boy cups his hands to his mouth and pipes: "Laahh-sie! Laahh-sie!" And then we see it – way out there at the end of the field – the ripple, the dashing furrow, the blur of the streaking dog, white chest, flashing feet.

1 **Colorado:** großer Fluss (2333 km) in den USA, der durch mehrere Staaten und den Grand Canyon fließt.
adolescence: Jugend.
4 **strains:** Klänge.
5 **mournful:** traurig, trauervoll, klagend.
7 **dismal:** trostlos.

Two Ships

I saw him today. At the side of the road, head down, walking. There were the full-leafed trees, the maples, elms, and oaks I see every day, the snarl of the wild berry bushes, sumac, milkweed, and thistle, the snaking hot macadam road, sun-flecked shadows. And him. An apparition: squat, bow-legged, in shorts, T-shirt, and sandals, his head shaved to the bone, biceps like legs of lamb. I slowed with the shock of seeing him there, with the recognition that worked in my ankles and fingertips like sap, and for a stunned second or two I stared, fixated, as the car pulled me closer and then swept past him in a rush. I was dressed in white, on my way to crack stinging serves and

3 **maple:** Ahorn.
4 **elm:** Ulme.
snarl: Gestrüpp.
5 **sumac:** Sumach (sommer- oder immergrüner Strauch).
milkweed: Schwalbenwurzgewächs.
thistle: Distel.
6 **macadam:** Schotter, Splitt.
7 **apparition:** Erscheinung.
squat: untersetzt.
bow-legged: o-beinig.
11 **sap:** Saft, Lebenskraft.
stunned: benommen, wie betäubt.
14 **to crack stinging serves:** gepfefferte Aufschläge liefern (Tennis) (*stinging:* [fig.] scharf).

return treacherous backhands in sweet arcing loops. He never looked up.

When I got home I made some phone calls. He was back in the country – legally – the government forgiving, his mind like damaged fruit. Thirty-one years old, he was staying with his parents, living in the basement, doing God knows what – strumming a guitar, lifting weights, putting pieces of wood together – the things he'd been doing since he was fourteen. Erica listened as I pried information from the receiver, a cigarette in the corner of her mouth, polished surfaces behind her.

I was pouring Haig & Haig over a hard white knot of ice cubes. The last of my informants had got off the subject of Casper and was filling me in on the pains in her neck, lips, toes, and groin as I cradled the receiver between ear and shoulder. The smile I gave Erica was weak. When the whiskey-cracked voice on the other end of the line paused to snatch a quick breath, I changed the subject, whispered a word of encouragement and hung up.

1 **treacherous backhands:** gefährliche Rückhandschläge (Tennis).
arcing: bogenförmig.
loop: Schleife, Bogen, Kurve.
7 **to strum s.th.:** auf etwas klimpern.
10 **to pry information:** Informationen entlocken.
13 **Haig & Haig:** bekannte Whisky-Marke.
15 **to fill s.o. in on s.th.:** jdn. über etwas aufklären, informieren, ins Bild setzen.
16 **groin:** Unterleib, Leistengegend.
to cradle s.th.: etwas festhalten.
19 **to snatch a quick breath:** schnell Luft holen.

"Well?" Erica was on her feet.

"We've got to move," I said.

I was overdramatizing. For effect. Overdramatizing because humor resides in exaggeration, and humor is a quick cover for alarm and bewilderment. I *was* alarmed. He could stay indefinitely, permanently. He could show up at the tennis courts, at the lake, at my front door. And then what would I do? Turn my back, look through him, crouch behind the door and listen to the interminable sharp intercourse of knuckle and wood?

"Is it really that bad?" Erica said.

I sipped at my Scotch and nodded. It was really that bad.

Twelve years ago we'd been friends. Close friends. We'd known each other from the dawn of consciousness on. We played in the cradle, in the schoolyard, went to camp together, listened to the same teachers, blocked and batted for the same teams. When we were sixteen we declared war on the bourgeois state and its material and canonical manifestations. That is,

5 **bewilderment:** Verwirrung.
6 **indefinitely** (adv.): auf unbestimmte Zeit.
9 **to crouch:** sich niederkauern.
10 **interminable:** endlos.
intercourse: Zusammenprall.
13 **to nod:** nicken.
17 **cradle:** Wiege.
19 **blocked and batted for the same team:** haben zusammen im gleichen Baseballteam gespielt.
21 **canonical manifestation:** Vorschrift.

we were horny adolescents sublimating glandular frustrations in the most vicious and mindless acts of vandalism. We smoked pot, gulped stolen vodka, and drove our parents' cars at a hundred miles an hour. Each night we cruised the back streets till three or four, assaulting religious statues, churches, the slick curvilinear windshields of Porsches and Cadillacs. Indiscriminate, we burned crosses and six-pointed stars. We tore down fences, smashed picture windows, filled Jacuzzis with sand. Once we climbed a treacherous three-hundred-foot cliff in utter darkness so we could drop raw eggs on the patrons of the chic restaurant nestled at its base. We committed secretive acts of defiance the way Crazy Horse counted coup. We lacked perspective.

---

1 **horny adolescent** (coll.): geile(r) Pubertierende(r), sexuell erregte(r) Jugendliche(r).
to sublimate: (einen unbefriedigten Trieb) umsetzen, (psychische oder sexuelle Energien) umleiten.
glandular: hormonell.
2 **vicious:** böse.
3 **pot:** Marihuana.
to gulp: gierig schlucken, runterstürzen.
6 **to assault:** angreifen.
7 **curvilinear:** gebogen, krummlinig.
7 f. **indiscriminate:** willkürlich, wahllos.
10 **Jacuzzi:** Whirlpool.
12 **patron:** (Restaurant-, Hotel-)Gast.
13 **nestled:** eingebettet, geschmiegt.
secretive: heimlich.
13 f. **act of defiance:** Trotzhandlung.
14 **Crazy Horse:** Häuptling des Sioux-Stammes (1842–77); bekannt für seinen Mut.

Casper saw the whole thing as a crusade. He was given to diatribe, and his diatribes had suddenly begun to bloom with the rhetoric of Marxism. We would annihilate a dentist's plaster lawn ornaments – flamingoes and lantern-wielding pickaninnies – and he'd call it class warfare. Privately, I saw our acts of destruction as a way of pissing in my father's eye.

We ran away from home at one point – I think we were fifteen or so – and it was then that I had my first intimation of just how fanatical and intransigent Casper could be. I'd never considered him abnormal, had never thought about it. There was his obsession with the bodily functions, the vehement disgust he felt over his parents' lovemaking – *I could hear them*, he would say, his features pinched with contempt, *grunting and slobbering, humping like pigs* – the fact that he went to a shrink twice a week. But none of this was very different from what other fifteen-year-olds did and said and felt, myself included. Now, running

1 **crusade:** Kreuzzug.
2 **to be given to s.th.:** zu etwas neigen.
diatribe: Schmährede.
4 **to annihilate:** vernichten.
plaster: Gips.
5 **lantern-wielding:** Laternen schwingend, schwenkend.
pickaninny (pej.): Negerkind.
10 **intimation:** Andeutung, Wink; Ahnung.
intransigent: unnachgiebig.
13 **disgust:** Ekel.
15 f. **to grunt:** grunzen.
16 **to slobber:** sabbern.
to hump (vulg.): Sex haben.
17 **shrink** (coll.): Seelenklempner(in).

away, I saw that Casper's behavior went beyond the pale of wise-guyism or healthy adolescent rebellion. I recognized the spark of madness in him, and I was both drawn to it and repelled by it. He was serious, he was committed, his was the rapture of saints and martyrs, both feet over the line. He went too far; I drew back from him.

We'd planned this excursion with all the secrecy and precision of prison breakers. Twenty miles away, tucked deep in the leafy recesses of Fahnestock State Park, was a huge cache of canned food, an ax, two sixpacks of Jaguar malt liquor, sleeping bags, and a tent. We signed in at school, ducked out the back door, hitchhiked the twenty miles, and experienced freedom. The following day, while we were exploring the park, my father stalked up to the campsite (my brother had broken down under interrogation and given us away) and settled down to wait. My father is

1 f. **to go beyond the pale:** (fig.) die Grenze(n) überschreiten.
2 **wise-guyism** (coll.): Klugscheißerei.
3 **spark:** Funke.
4 **to be repelled by s.th.:** von etwas abgestoßen, angewidert sein.
5 **rapture:** Entzücken.
6 **both feet over the line** (fig.): deutlich zu weit gehend.
10 **recess:** Winkel, Nische.
10 f. **Fahnestock State Park:** Nationalpark in der Nähe von New York mit einer Größe von 400 km^2.
11 **cache:** (Proviant-)Lager.
12 **sixpack:** Sechserpack(ung) (Bier).
malt liquor: aus Malz gebrautes alkoholisches Getränk, Starkbier.
13 **to duck out s.th.** (coll.): aus etwas türmen.
16 **to stalk up to s.th.:** sich an etwas heranpirschen.
17 **interrogation:** Verhör.
18 **to give s.o. away:** jdn. verraten.

a powerful and unforgiving man. He tapped a birch switch against a rock for an hour, then packed up everything he could carry – food, tent, sleeping bags, canteens – and hiked out to the highway. The sight of the barren campsite made by blood leap. At first I thought we were in the wrong spot, the trees all alike, dusk falling, but then Casper pointed out the blackened circle of rocks we'd cooked a triumphant dinner over the night before. I found my father's note pinned to a tree. It was curt and minatory, the script an angry flail.

Casper refused to give in. Between us we had four dollars and twenty cents. He dragged me through swamps and brambles, the darkening stalks of the trees, past ponds, down hills, and out to the highway. Afraid to hitch – my father could be glaring behind each pair of headlights – we skirted the road and made our way to a clapboard grocery where we purchased a twenty-five-pound bag of Ken-L Ration. Outside, it was 29° F. We hiked back up into the

1 f. **birch switch:** Birkenrute.
4 **canteen:** Feldflasche.
7 **dusk:** Abenddämmerung.
10 **curt:** kurz, knapp.
minatory: drohend, bedrohlich.
11 **flail:** Dreschen.
14 **swamp:** Sumpf.
brambles: dornige Sträucher.
stalk: hier: Baumstamm.
16 **to glare:** zornig starren.
17 **to skirt s.th.:** etwas umgehen.
18 **clapboard:** Schindel.
19 **Ken-L Ration:** Handelsname eines Hundefutters.

woods, drank from a swamp, crunched the kibbled nuggets of glyceryl monostearate and animal fat preserved with BHA, and slept in our jackets. In the morning I slipped away, walked out to the road, and hitchhiked back home.

The state police were called in to track Casper down. They employed specially trained trackers and bloodhounds. Casper's parents hired a helicopter search team for eighty-five dollars an hour. The helicopter spotted Casper twice. Whirring, kicking up a cyclone, the machine hovered over the treetops while Casper's mother shouted stentorian pleas through a bullhorn. He ran. Two weeks later he turned up at home, in bed, asleep.

It was just after this that Casper began to talk incessantly of repression and the police state. He shuffled round the corridors at school with a huge, distended satchel full of poorly printed pamphlets in

1 **to crunch:** knabbern.
kibbled: gemahlen.
2 **nugget:** Klumpen.
glyceryl monostearate: Zusatzstoff in der Lebensmittelindustrie mit der Bezeichnung E471.
3 **BHA:** Abk. für *butylated hydroxyanisole:* Konservierungsstoff für fetthaltige Lebensmittel.
10 **to whirr:** schwirren, surren.
11 **cyclone:** Zyklon, Wirbelsturm.
to hover: schweben.
12 **stentorian:** schallend.
13 **bullhorn:** Megaphon.
15 f. **incessantly** (adv.): unaufhörlich.
16 **repression:** Unterdrückung.
17 **to shuffle:** schlurfen.
18 **distended satchel:** voll gestopfte Schultasche.

faded greens and grays: *The Speeches of V. I. Lenin, State and Anarchy, Das Kapital.* The rhetoric never appealed to me, but the idea of throwing off the yoke, of discounting and discrediting all authority, was a breath of fresh air.

He quit college at nineteen and went to live among the revolutionary workers of the Meachum Brothers Tool & Die Works in Queens. Six months later he was drafted. How they accepted him or why he agreed to report, I'll never know. He was mad as a loon, fixated in his Marxist-Leninist phase, gibbering nonstop about imperialist aggressors and the heroic struggle of the revolutionary democratic peoples of the Republic of Vietnam. It was summer. I was living in Lake George with Erica and he came up for a day or two before they inducted him.

He was worked up – I could see that the minute he got off the bus. His feet shuffled, but his limbs and torso danced, elbows jerking as if they were wired, the big knapsack trembling on his back, a cord pulsing under his left eye. He was wearing a cap that clung to his head like something alive, and the first thing he did was remove it with a flourish to show off

3 **yoke:** Joch.
4 **to discount:** unberücksichtigt lassen.
9 **to draft s.o.:** jdn. zum Militär einziehen.
10 **loon:** Blödmann.
11 **to gibber:** (daher)plappern.
16 **to induct:** (zum Militär) einziehen, einberufen.
17 **to be worked up:** aufgeregt sein.
19 **to jerk:** zucken.
20 **knapsack:** Tornister.
23 **flourish:** schwungvolle Bewegung.

his bald scalp: he'd shaved himself – denuded himself – every hair plucked out, right down to his mustache and eyebrows. From the neck up he looked like a space invader; from the neck down, rigidly muscled, he was Charles Atlas.

He couldn't stop talking. Couldn't sit down, couldn't sleep, couldn't eat. Said he was going into the army all right, but that he'd do everything in his power to subvert them, and that when they shipped him to Vietnam he'd turn his weapon on his own platoon and then join the NLF. I tried to joke with him, distract him – if only for a moment. But he was immovable. He played his one note till Erica and I just wanted to jump into the car and leave him there with the house, the books, the stereo, everything. Someone pulled a knife out of my ribs when he left.

I never saw him again. Until today.

Rumor had it that he'd disappeared from Fort Dix the first week. He was in Canada, he was in Sweden. The Finns had jailed him for entering the country illegally, the Swiss had expelled him. He was in Belize City stirring up the locals, the British had got hold of

1 **to denude o.s.:** sich entblößen.
5 **Atlas:** Charles A., d. i. Angelo Siciliano (1893–1972), bekannter US-Bodybuilder; Sohn italienischer Einwanderer.
9 **to subvert:** unterwandern.
10 f. **platoon:** Zug, Einheit, Truppe.
11 **NLF:** Abk. für *National Liberation Front:* Bund der kommunistischen Dissidenten in Süd-Vietnam, gegründet 1960.
12 **to distract:** ablenken, auf andere Gedanken bringen.
18 **Fort Dix:** Ausbildungslager der US-Armee in New Jersey.
21 **to expel s.o.:** jdn. ausweisen.
21 f. **Belize City:** Hauptstadt von Belize (ehemals British Honduras).

him and the United States was pressing for his extradition. Rumors. They sifted back to me through my mother, friends, people who claimed they'd seen him or talked to someone who had. I was in law school, student-deferred. There were exams, the seasons changed, Erica visited on weekends, and there were long breathy phone calls in between. In my second year, the packages began to show up in my mailbox. Big, crudely bundled manuscripts – manuscripts the size of phone books – sent from an address in London, Ontario.

There were no cover letters. But, then, cover letters would have been superfluous: the moment I saw the crabbed scrawl across the flat surface of the first package (lettering so small it could have been written with the aid of magnification), I knew who had sent it. Inside these packages were poems. Or, rather, loosely organized snatches of enjambed invective in strident upper-case letters:

2 **extradition:** Auslieferung.
to sift back to s.o.: etwa: erneut zu jdm. durchdringen.
5 **student-deferred:** als Student vom Militärdienst (in Vietnam) befreit.
7 **breathy:** hauchig.
12 **cover letter:** Begleitbrief.
13 **superfluous:** überflüssig.
14 **crabbed scrawl:** unleserliches Gekritzel.
16 **aid of magnification:** Vergrößerungshilfe, Lupe.
18 **snatches of enjambed invective:** Bruchstücke ununterbrochener Schimpfwörter, Schimpfkanonade.
strident: durchdringend, grell.
19 **upper-case letters:** Großbuchstaben.

THE FASCIST NAZI ABORTIONIST LOBBY THAT FEEDS
ON THE TATTERED FLESH OF ASIAN ORPHANS
MUST BE CIRCUMVENTED FROM ITS IMPERIALIST EXPANSIONIST DESIGN
TO ENSLAVE THE MASSES AND TURN ARTIFICIALLY NATIONALIZED
PROLETARIANS AGAINST BROTHER AND SISTER PROLETARIANS
IN THE INTERNECINE CONFLICT THAT FEEDS
THE COFFERS
OF THE REVISIONIST RUNNING DOGS
OF BOURGEOIS COMPLACENCY!

The poems went on for hundreds of pages. I couldn't read them. I wondered why he had sent them to me. Was he trying to persuade me? Was he trying to justify himself, reach out, recapture some sympathy he'd deluded himself into thinking we'd once shared? I was in law school. I didn't know what to do. Eventually, the packages stopped coming.

Erica and I married, moved back to Westchester,

1 **abortionist** (pej.): hier etwa: Missgeburt.
3 **tattered:** zerfetzt.
orphan: Waise.
4 **to circumvent s.o. from s.th.:** jdn. von etwas abbringen.
10 **internecine:** für beide Seiten verlustreich.
11 **coffer:** Geldtruhe.
12 **running dog:** Lakai.
13 **complacency:** Selbstzufriedenheit.
17 **to recapture:** wiedererlangen.
18 **to delude o.s. into doing s.th.:** sich dazu verleiten lassen, etwas zu tun.
21 **Westchester:** Verwaltungsbezirk im Bundesstaat New York.

built a house, had a daughter. I was working in a law firm in White Plains. One night, 2:00 A.M., the phone rang. It was Casper. "Jack," he said, "it's me, Casper. Listen, listen, this is important, this is vital –" Phone calls in the night. I hadn't spoken to him in seven years, gulfs had opened between us, I was somebody else – and yet here he was, with the same insistent, demanding voice that wraps you up in unasked-for intimacies like a boa constrictor, talking as if we'd just seen each other the day before. I sat up. He was nearly crying.

"Jack: you've got to do something for me, life and death, you got to promise me –"

"Wait a minute," I said, "wait, hold on –" I didn't want to hear it. I was angry, puzzled; I had to be at work in five and a half hours.

"Just this one thing. You know me, right? Just this: if anybody asks, you stick up for me, okay? No, no: I mean, tell them I'm all right, you know what I mean? That I'm good. There's nothing wrong with me, understand?"

What could I say? The phone went dead, the room was dark. Beside me, in bed, Erica shifted position and let out a sigh that would have soothed all the renegades in the world.

2 **White Plains:** Stadt im Bundesstaat New York, etwa 25 Meilen nördlich von Manhattan.
6 **gulf:** Kluft, Abgrund.
7 **insistent:** ein-, aufdringlich, nachdrücklich.
18 **to stick up for s.o.:** für jdn. eintreten, zu jdm. halten.
24 **to soothe:** beruhigen.
24 f. **renegade:** Abtrünnige(r).

I was busy. The incident slipped my mind. Three days later a man in an elaborately buckled and belted trench coat stepped into the anteroom at Hermening & Stinson, the firm that had given me my tenuous foothold in the world of corporate law. No one paid much attention to him until he announced that he was from the FBI and that he wanted to speak with me. The typist stopped typing. Charlie Hermening looked up at me like a barn owl scanning the rafters. I shrugged my shoulders.

The man was big and fleshy and pale, his irises like water, wisps of white hair peeping out from beneath the fedora that hugged his bullet head. When I showed him into my office he flashed his credentials, and I remember wondering if TV producers had studied FBI men, or if FBI men had learned how to act from watching TV. He took a seat, but declined to remove either his hat or trench coat. Was I acquainted with a Casper R. Hansen, he wanted to know. Did I know his whereabouts? When had I seen him last?

2 **buckled:** zugeschnallt.
3 **anteroom:** Vorzimmer.
4 **tenuous:** unsicher, anfällig.
5 **corporate law:** Unternehmens-, Gesellschaftsrecht.
9 **barn owl:** Schleiereule.
rafters (pl.): (Dach-)Sparren.
10 **to shrug one's shoulders:** die Achseln zucken.
12 **wisp:** (Haar-)Strähne, Büschel.
to peep out: hervorlugen.
13 **fedora:** Filzhut.
to hug s.th.: dicht an etwas anliegen, etwas fest umschließen.
14 **credentials:** Ausweispapiere.

Had he telephoned, sent anything in the mail? What did I think of his mental state?

"His mental state?" I repeated.

"Yes," the man said, soft and articulate as a professor, "I want to know if you feel he's mentally competent."

I thought about it for a minute, thought about Lake George, the poems, Casper's tense and frightened voice over the phone. I almost asked the FBI man why he wanted to know: Was Casper in trouble? Had he done something illegal? I wanted to gauge the man's response, listen for nuances that might give me a clue as to what I should say. But I didn't. I simply leaned across the desk, looked the man in the eye, and told him that in my estimation Casper was seriously impaired.

That was a year ago. I'd forgotten the man from the FBI, forgotten Casper. Until now. Now he was back. Like a slap in the face, like a pointed finger: he was back.

"What are you afraid of?" Erica asked. "That he'll say hello or shake your hand or something?"

It was dark. Moths batted against the screens; I toyed with my asparagus crêpes and spinach salad. The baby was in bed. I poured another glass of French Colombard. "No," I said, "that's not it." And

11 **to gauge:** beurteilen.
16 **impaired:** beeinträchtigt.
23 **moth:** Nachtfalter.
24 **asparagus:** Spargel.
26 **French Colombard:** kalifornischer Wein.

then: "Yes. That would be bad enough. Think of the embarrassment."

"Embarrassment? You were friends, you grew up together."

"Yes," I said. That was the problem. I sipped at the wine.

"Look, I'm not exactly thrilled about seeing him either – the weekend at Lake George was enough to last me a lifetime – but it's not the end of the world or anything. … I mean, nothing says you've got to invite him over for dinner so he can lecture us on the wisdom of Mao Tse-tung or tell us how miserable he is."

She was in the kitchen area, spooning the foam off a cup of cappuccino. "Are you afraid he'll vandalize the house – is that it?"

"I don't know," I said. "I mean, we're not kids any more – he's not that crazy." I thought about it, listening to the hiss of the coffee maker. The house we'd put up was pretty cozy and dramatic. Modern. With decks and skylights and weathered wood and huge sheets of glass. It called attention to itself, stylish and unique, a cut above the slant-roofed cottages that lined the road. It was precisely the sort of house

12 **Mao Tse-tung:** Führer der chinesischen Kommunistischen Partei und erster Staatsführer der Volksrepublik China (1893–1976).
14 **to vandalize:** mutwillig beschädigen.
18 **hiss:** Zischen.
19 **dramatic:** hier: auffallend, außergewöhnlich.
20 **deck:** Sonnenterrasse.
skylight: Dachfenster.
22 **a cut above:** um einiges überlegen.
slant-roofed: mit Schrägdach.

Casper and I had sought out and violated when we were sixteen. I looked up from my wine. "He might," I admitted.

Erica looked alarmed. "Should we call the police?"

"Don't be ridiculous, we can't –" I broke off. It was futile. I wasn't really afraid of that sort of thing – no, my fears went deeper, deeper than I wanted to admit. He would look at me and he would condemn me: I'd become what we'd reacted against together, what he'd devoted his mad, misguided life to subverting. That was the problem. That's why I didn't want to see him at the tennis courts or at the lake or even walking along the road with his shoulders hunched under the weight of his convictions.

"Hey" – she was at my side, massaging the back of my neck – "why not forget about it, you've got enough worries as it is." She was right. The EPA was filing suit against one of our clients – a battery company accused of dumping toxic waste in the Hudson – and I'd been poring over the regulations looking for some sort of loophole. I was meeting with Charlie

1 **to violate:** verschandeln.
6 **futile:** nutzlos.
10 **misguided:** töricht, unsinnig.
13 **hunched:** gebeugt.
17 **EPA:** Abk. für *Environmental Protection Agency:* Staatliche Umweltbehörde der USA.
18 **to file suit:** Anklage erheben.
19 **to dump:** abladen, kippen.
toxic waste: Giftmüll.
Hudson: *Hudson River:* Fluss in New York.
20 **to pore over s.th.:** über etwas brüten, etwas eifrig studieren.
21 **loophole:** Lücke im Gesetz.

Hermening in the morning to show him what I'd come up with.

"You know something – didn't Rose say he'd been back nearly a month already?" She was purring, the cappuccino smelled like a feast, I could feel the alcohol loosening my knotted nerves. "And you only saw him today for the first time? If he was going to come over, wouldn't he have done it by now?"

I was about to admit she was right, finish my coffee, and take a look at the newspaper when there was a knock at the door. A knock at the door. It was nine-thirty. I nearly kicked the table over. "I'm not here," I hissed. "No matter who it is," and I slipped into the bedroom.

There were voices in the hallway. I heard Erica, and then the polite but vaguely querulous tones of – a woman? – and then Erica's voice, projecting: "Jack. Jack, will you come out here, please?"

Mrs. Shapiro, our next-door neighbor, was standing in the doorway. "Sorry to bother you," the old woman said, "but your garbitch is all over the driveway – I can't even get the car through."

Garbage? Her driveway was at least fifty feet from ours. What was she talking about?

4 **to purr:** schnurren.
6 **knotted:** verkrampft.
13 **to hiss:** zischen.
16 **querulous:** nörglerisch, missmutig.
17 **projecting:** laut und deutlich (Stimme).
21 **garbitch:** *garbage.*

The night was warm, redolent of flowers and grass clippings. There was a moon, and the crickets seemed to be serenading it, chirring in the trees like a steel band locked in a groove. I walked beside Mrs. Shapiro to where her car sat rumbling and sputtering, lights flooding the gumbo of vegetable peels, papers, milk cartons, and diapers strewn across her driveway. The cans had been deliberately hauled down the street, upended and dumped – no dog or raccoon could have been so determined or efficient. This was deliberate. As I bent to the mess, I thought of Casper.

"Kids." Mrs. Shapiro, arms folded, stood silhouetted against the headlights. She spat the words out as if she were cursing. "Things just seem to get worse and worse, don't they?"

I worked in silence, embarrassed, digging into the slop with my bare hands, trying not to think about baby stool, maggots, the yielding wet paste of coffee

1 *(to be)* **redolent of s.th.:** nach etwas duften.
1f. **grass clippings** (pl.): gemähtes Gras.
2 **cricket:** Grille.
3 **to serenade:** ein Ständchen bringen.
to chirr: zirpen.
4 **groove:** Rille (einer Schallplatte).
5 **to rumble:** dröhnen, rumpeln, poltern.
to sputter: stottern (Motor).
6 **gumbo:** hier: (fig.) Suppe, Brühe.
7 **diaper:** Windel.
8 **to haul s.th.:** etwas schleppen.
9 **upended:** umgedreht, auf den Kopf gestellt.
raccoon: Waschbär.
17 **slop:** Schmutz.
18 **baby stool:** Babystuhlgang.
maggot: Made.

grounds and canteloupe shells, scooping it up by the armload. When I was finished I told Mrs. Shapiro that I'd have Erica hose down the driveway for her in the morning. The elderly woman merely raised her hand as if to say "Forget about it," tumbled into the car seat, and set the car in motion with a shriek of the steering mechanism and a rumble of rotten exhaust. I watched the taillights trace the arc of her driveway, then hauled the garbage cans back to my own yard, all the while expecting Casper to pop out at me with a laugh. Or maybe he was crouching in the bushes, giggling to himself like a half-witted adolescent. That was about his speed, I thought.

Inside, I washed up, fumed at Erica – "It was deliberate," I kept saying, "I know it was" – and then shut myself up in the study with the brief I'd prepared on the battery manufacturer. I couldn't read a word of it. After a while – it must have been twenty minutes or so – I heard Erica getting ready for bed – running water, brushing her teeth – and then the house went silent. I knew I should go over the brief a couple of

1 **canteloupe:** Honigmelone.
to scoop s.th. up: etwas aufschaufeln.
3 **to hose s.th. down:** etwas (mit dem Wasserschlauch) abspritzen.
6 **shriek:** Kreischen.
8 **taillight:** Rücklicht.
arc: (Kreis-)Bogen.
12 **to giggle:** kichern.
half-witted: schwachsinnig.
12f. **that was about his speed** (coll.): das sah ihm ganz ähnlich.
14 **to fume at s.o.:** wütend sein mit jdm.
16 **brief:** Darlegung der Beweisgründe.

times, have a mug of hot Ovaltine, and get a good night's rest. But I was rooted to the chair, thinking about Casper – a grown man, thirty-one years old – sneaking around in the dark dumping people's garbage. What could he be thinking of?

A muffled sound was pulsing through the house. At first it didn't register, and then, with a flash of anger, I realized what it was: someone was knocking at the door. This was too much. If there was garbage in the neighbors' driveway they could damn well clean it up themselves, I thought, storming down the hallway. I wrenched the door back, expecting Mrs. Shapiro.

It was Casper.

He stood there, his head bowed, the moon blanching the stiff bristle of his crown. He was wearing a sleeveless T-shirt, shorts, sandals. The veins stood out in his arms. When he looked up at me his eyes were soft and withdrawn. "Jack," was all he said.

I was at a loss. The worst possible scenario was playing itself out on my doorstep, and I was caught up in it, against my will, suddenly forced to take a part. I felt like an unrehearsed actor shoved out onstage; I felt exhausted and defeated. My initial impulse had been to slam the door shut, but now, with Casper

4 **to sneak around:** herumschleichen.
6 **muffled:** gedämpft.
7 **not to register:** keinen Eindruck machen.
12 **to wrench the door back:** die Tür aufreißen.
14 f. **to blanch:** bleichen.
15 **bristle:** Stoppel(n).
crown: Scheitel.
22 **to shove:** schieben.

standing there before me, I could only clear my throat, wipe my features clean, and ask him in.

He hesitated. "No," he said, "no, I couldn't do that. I mean, I just came to … to say hello, that's all."

"Don't be silly," I said, insistent, already ushering him in. "Here, the living room. Have a seat. Can I get you something: beer? brandy? 7-Up?"

We were standing beside each other in the center of the living room. He took in the potted plants, the umbrella tree, the little Paul Klee my mother had given me. The nearest piece of furniture was the loveseat; he perched on the edge of it, apologetic. "No thanks," he said, eyes on the floor.

I was halfway to the kitchen, needing a brandy. "You sure? It's no trouble at all. I've got liqueur – how about a Drambuie?" It had suddenly become crucially important that I give him something, an offering of some sort, a peace pipe, the communal leg of lamb. "Are you hungry? I've got Brie and crackers – I could make a sandwich –?"

He was still staring at the floor. "Milk," he said, so softly I wasn't sure I'd heard him.

1 f. **I could only … wipe my features clean:** ich konnte nur ein unbeteiligtes Gesicht machen.
5 **to usher:** geleiten.
9 **to take s.th. in:** etwas wahrnehmen, registrieren.
10 **umbrella tree:** amerikanische Magnolienart.
11 f. **loveseat:** S-förmiges Sofa.
12 **to perch:** hocken, thronen.
apologetic: zaghaft, bescheiden.
16 **Drambuie:** schottischer Whiskylikör.
18 f. **communal leg of lamb** (fig.): gemeinschaftliches Mahl zur Feier einer Rückkehr.

"You want a glass of milk?"

"Yes, thanks – if it's not too much trouble."

I made some deprecatory noises, poured out a brandy and a milk, arranged some Danish flatbread on a platter around the cheese. Two minutes later we were sitting across the room from each other. I was looking into my brandy snifter; he was studying the glass of milk as if he'd never seen anything like it before. "So," I said, "you're back."

He didn't answer. Just sat there, looking at his milk. There was something monkish about him – perhaps it was the crewcut. I thought of acolytes, nuns, the crop-headed Hare Krishnas in airport lounges. "It's been a long time," I offered. No response. It occurred to me to ask about the garbage cans – perhaps we could share the intimacy of the joke – but then I thought better of it: no sense in embarrassing him or stirring up any rancor.

"About the garbage cans," he said, as if reading my thoughts, "I did it."

I waited for an explanation. He stared at me so fixedly I finally looked away, and more as a means of breaking the silence than satisfying my curiosity, I asked him why.

3 **deprecatory:** missbilligend.
7 **snifter:** (Kognac-)Schwenker.
12 **crewcut:** Bürstenschnitt.
acolyte: Messdiener.
12f. **crop-headed:** mit extrem kurzen Haaren, Stutzkopf-.
13 **Hare Krishnas** (pl.): Anhänger der Religionsgemeinschaft, die den Lehren von Bhaktivedanta Swami Prabhupada folgt.
18 **rancor:** Bitterkeit, Groll.

He seemed to consider this. "I don't know," he said finally, took a tentative sip of milk, then downed the glass in a single gulp. He belched softly and settled back in the chair.

I was losing my patience. I had work in the morning. The last thing I wanted to do was sit here with this wacko, on edge in my own living room, mouthing the little platitudes of social formality when I knew both of us were seething. I made another stab at conversation, just because the silence was so inadmissible. "So," I said, "we've wondered about you from time to time, Erica and I. … We have a daughter, did you know that? Her name's Tricia."

His arms were rigid, tense with muscle. He was staring down at his interlocked fingers, straining with the tension, as if he were doing an isometric exercise. "I was in the hospital," he said.

The hospital. The syllables bit into me, made something race round the edge of my stomach. I did not want to hear it.

I got up to pour another brandy. "More milk?" I

2 **tentative:** vorsichtig, zögernd.
2f. **to down s.th. in a single gulp:** etwas in einem Zug austrinken, herunterkippen.
3 **to belch:** rülpsen.
7 **wacko** (coll.): Verrückte(r).
on edge: nervös, gereizt.
8 **platitudes:** Platitüden, Plattheiten.
9 **to seethe:** (fig.) kochen.
stab: Versuch.
10f. **inadmissible:** unzulässig.
15 **interlocked:** ineinander verschränkt.

asked, the rigorous host, but he ignored me. He was going to tell me about the hospital. He raised his voice so I could hear him.

"They said it was a condition of giving me a clean slate. You know, they'd rehabilitate me. Eleven months. Locked up with the shit-flingers and droolers, the guys they'd shot up in the war. That was the hospital."

I stood in the kitchen doorway, the brandy in my hand. He was accusing me. I'd started the war, oppressed the masses, wielded the dollar like an ax; I'd deserted him, told the FBI the truth, created the American Nazi Party, and erected the slums, stick by stick. What did he want from me – to say I was sorry? Sorry he was crazy, sorry he couldn't go to law school, sorry Marx's venom had eaten away the inside of his brain?

He was on his feet now. The empty glass flashed in his hand as he crossed the room. He handed it to me. We were inches apart. "Jack," he said. I looked away.

"I've got to go now," he whispered.

I stood at the door and watched him recede into the moonlight that spilled across the lawn like milk. He turned left on the macadam road, heading in the direction of his parents' house.

1 **rigorous:** rigoros, streng, strikt.
4f. **clean slate** (coll.): reine Weste.
6 **shit-flinger** (vulg.): Dreckschleuder.
drooler: Mensch, der sabbert.
10f. **to oppress:** unterdrücken.
16 **venom:** Gift.
22 **to recede:** sich entfernen.

Erica was behind me in her robe, squinting against the light in the hallway. "Jack?" she said.

I barely heard her. Standing there in the doorway, watching the shadows close like a fist over the lawn, I was already packing.

1 **robe:** Morgenrock, Bademantel.
to squint: blinzeln.

Sinking House

When Monty's last breath caught somewhere in the back of his throat with a sound like the tired wheeze of an old screen door, the first thing she did was turn on the water. She leaned over him a minute to make sure, then she wiped her hands on her dress and shuffled into the kitchen. Her fingers trembled as she jerked at the lever and felt the water surge against the porcelain. Steam rose in her face; a glitter of liquid leapt for the drain. Croak, that's what they called it. Now she knew why. She left the faucet running in the kitchen and crossed the gloomy expanse of the living room, swung down the hallway to the guest bedroom, and turned on both taps in the bathroom there. It was almost as an afterthought that she decided to fill the tub too.

3 **wheeze:** Keuchen, Schnaufen, Pfeifen.
4 **screen door:** Tür mit Fliegengitter.
7 **to shuffle:** schlurfen.
8 **to jerk at the lever:** den Hebel ruckartig umlegen, öffnen.
to surge: strömen.
9 **glitter:** Glitzern.
10 **drain:** Abfluss(rohr).
croak: Krächzen; (coll.) Abkratzen.
11 **faucet:** Wasserhahn.
12 **gloomy:** dunkel, düster.
expanse: Fläche.

For a long while she sat in the leather armchair in the living room. The sound of running water – pure, baptismal, as uncomplicated as the murmur of a brook in Vermont or a toilet at the Waldorf – soothed her. It trickled and trilled, burbling from either side of the house and driving down the terrible silence that crouched in the bedroom over the lifeless form of her husband.

The afternoon was gone and the sun plunging into the canopy of the big eucalyptus behind the Finkelsteins' when she finally pushed herself up from the chair. Head down, arms moving stiffly at her sides, she scuffed out the back door, crossed the patio, and bent to turn on the sprinklers. They sputtered and spat – not enough pressure, that much she understood – but finally came to life in halfhearted umbrellas of mist. She left the hose trickling in the rose garden, then went back into the house, passed through

3 **baptismal:** die Taufe betreffend.
4 **brook:** Bach.
Vermont: Bundesstaat im Nordosten der USA.
Waldorf: exklusive Hotelkette.
to soothe: beruhigen.
5 **to trickle:** tröpfeln, rinnen, rieseln.
to trill: trillern.
to burble: plätschern, gurgeln.
7 **to crouch:** hocken, kauern.
9 **to plunge:** tauchen.
10 **canopy:** Baldachin.
13 **to scuff:** schlurren, schlurfen.
patio: Veranda, Terrasse.
14 **sprinkler:** Rasensprenger, Berieselungsanlage.
to sputter: sprudeln, aufspritzen.

the living room, the kitchen, the master bedroom – not even a glance for Monty, no: she wouldn't look at him, not yet – and on into the master bath. The taps were weak, barely a trickle, but she left them on anyway, then flushed the toilet and pinned down the float with the brick Monty had used as a doorstop. And then finally, so weary she could barely lift her arms, she leaned into the stall and flipped on the shower.

Two weeks after the ambulance came for the old man next door, Meg Terwilliger was doing her stretching exercises on the prayer rug in the sunroom, a menthol cigarette glowing in the ashtray on the floor beside her, the new CD by Sandee and the Sharks thumping out of the big speakers in the corners. Meg was twenty-three, with the fine bones and haunted eyes of a poster child. She wore her black hair cut close at the temples, long in front, and she used a sheeny black eyeshadow to bring out the hunger in her eyes. In half an hour she'd have to pick up Tiffany at nursery school, drop off the dog at the veterinarian's, take Sonny's shirts to the cleaner's, buy a pound and a half

1 **master bedroom:** großes Schlafzimmer.
4 **trickle:** Rinnsal.
5 **to pin down the float:** den Schwimmer im Spülkasten herunterdrücken, befestigen.
8 **to flip s.th. on:** etwas aufdrehen, anmachen.
11 **sunroom:** verglaste Veranda.
13 **to thump:** dröhnen, hämmern.
15 **haunted:** gehetzt (Blick).
17 **sheeny:** glänzend.
20 **veterinarian:** Tierarzt.

of thresher shark, cilantro, and flour tortillas at the market, and start the burritos for supper. But now, she was stretching.

She took a deep drag on the cigarette, tugged at her right foot, and brought it up snug against her buttocks. After a moment she released it and drew back her left foot in its place. One palm flat on the floor, her head bobbing vaguely to the beat of the music, she did half a dozen repetitions, then paused to relight her cigarette. It wasn't until she turned over to do her straight-leg lifts that she noticed the dampness in the rug.

Puzzled, she rose to her knees and reached behind her to rub at the twin wet spots on the seat of her sweats. She lifted the corner of the rug, suspecting the dog, but there was no odor of urine. Looking closer, she saw that the concrete floor was a shade darker beneath the rug, as if it were bleeding moisture as it sometimes did in the winter. But this wasn't winter, this was high summer in Los Angeles and it hadn't rained for months. Cursing Sonny – he'd promised her ceramic tile and though she'd run all over town to get the

1 **thresher shark:** Drescherhai (tropischer Hochseefisch).
cilantro: Koriander.
2 **burrito** (Mex. Span.): gerollte Tortilla mit Füllung.
4 **to tug at s.th.:** an etwas ziehen.
5 **snug:** eng angelegt, dicht.
5f. **buttocks** (pl.): Gesäß, Hintern.
8 **to bob:** sich auf und ab bewegen.
11 **straight-leg lift:** Heben des ausgestreckten Beines.
15 **sweats** (pl.): Jogginghose.
18 **moisture:** Feuchtigkeit.
22 **tile:** Fliese(n).

best price on a nice Italian floral pattern, he still hadn't found the time to go look at it – she shot back the sliding door and stepped into the yard to investigate.

Immediately, she felt the Bermuda grass squelch beneath the soles of her aerobic shoes. She hadn't taken three strides – the sun in her face, Queenie yapping frantically from the fenced-in pool area – and her feet were wet. Had Sonny left the hose running? Or Tiffany? She slogged across the lawn, the pastel Reeboks spattered with wet, and checked the hose. It was innocently coiled on its tender, the tap firmly shut. Queenie's yapping went up an octave. The heat – it must have been ninety-five, a hundred – made her feel faint. She gazed up into the cloudless sky, then bent to check each of the sprinklers in succession.

She was poking around in the welter of bushes along the fence, looking for an errant sprinkler, when she thought of the old lady next door – Muriel, wasn't

2f. **sliding door:** Schiebetür.
3 **to investigate:** nachsehen, Nachforschungen anstellen.
4 **Bermuda grass:** auf Rasenflächen und Weiden im Süden der USA häufige niedrige Grasart.
to squelch: patschen, platschen.
6 **stride:** Schritt.
6f. **to yap:** kläffen.
7 **frantically** (adv.): wie wild.
9 **to slog:** sich mit schweren Schritten bewegen.
10 **spattered:** bespritzt.
11 **tender:** Schlauchrolle, -befestigung.
14 **to gaze:** blicken, starren.
16 **to poke around:** herumstochern.
welter: wirre Masse.
17 **errant:** verirrt.

that her name? What with her husband dying and all, maybe she'd left the hose running and forgotten all about it. Meg rose on her tiptoes to peer over the redwood fence that separated her yard from the neighbors' and found herself looking into a glistening, sunstruck garden, with banks of impatiens, bird of paradise, oleander, and loquat, roses in half a dozen shades. The sprinklers were on and the hose was running. For a long moment Meg stood there, mesmerized by the play of light through the drifting fans of water; she was wondering what it would be like to be old, thinking of how it would be if Sonny died and Tiffany were grown up and gone. She'd probably forget to turn off the sprinklers too.

The moment passed. The heat was deadening, the dog hysterical. Meg knew she would have to do something about the sodden yard and wet floor in the sunroom, but she dreaded facing the old woman. What would she say – I'm sorry your husband died but could you turn off the sprinklers? She was thinking maybe she'd phone – or wait till Sonny got home and let him handle it – when she stepped back from the fence and sank to her ankles in mud.

3 **on tiptoes:** auf Zehenspitzen.
to peer: spähen.
3f. **redwood:** Rotholz (vom Mammutbaum).
5 **glistening:** glitzernd, glänzend.
6 **impatiens:** Springkraut.
6f. **bird of paradise:** Paradiesvogelblume (beliebte Schnittblume).
7 **loquat:** Mispel.
9f. **mesmerized:** hypnotisiert, fasziniert.
17 **sodden:** durchnässt.

When the doorbell rang, Muriel was staring absently at the cover of an old *National Geographic* which lay beneath a patina of dust on the coffee table. The cover photo showed the beige and yellow sands of some distant desert, rippled to the horizon with corrugations that might have been waves on a barren sea. Monty was dead and buried. She wasn't eating much. Or sleeping much either. The sympathy cards sat unopened on the table in the kitchen, where the tap overflowed the sink and water plunged to the floor with a pertinacity that was like a redemption. When it was quiet – in the early morning or late at night – she could distinguish the separate taps, each with its own voice and rhythm, as they dripped and trickled from the far corners of the house. In those suspended hours she could make out the comforting gurgle of the toilet in the guest room, the musical wash of the tub as water cascaded over the lip of its porcelain dam, the quickening rush of the stream in the hallway as it shot like a miniature Niagara down the chasm of the floor vent … she could hear the drip

3 **patina:** Schicht.
5 **rippled:** gekräuselt.
5 f. **corrugations:** Furchen, Wellen.
6 **barren:** karg.
10 **to plunge:** stürzen.
11 **pertinacity:** Beharrlichkeit.
redemption: Erlösung, Rettung.
16 **suspended:** hier etwa: untätig, still.
18 **to cascade:** in Kaskaden herabstürzen, sich in Kaskaden ergießen.
21 **chasm:** Kluft, Abgrund.
vent: Öffnung.

in the master bedroom, the distant hiss of a shower, and the sweet eternal sizzle of the sprinklers on the back lawn.

But now she heard the doorbell.

Wearily, gritting her teeth against the pain in her lower legs and the damp lingering ache of her feet, she pushed herself up from the chair and sloshed her way to the door. The carpet was black with water, soaked through like a sponge – and in a tidy corner of her mind she regretted it – but most of the runoff was finding its way to the heating vents and the gaps in the corners where Monty had miscalculated the angle of the baseboard. She heard it dripping somewhere beneath the house and for a moment pictured the water lying dark and still in a shadowy lagoon that held the leaking ship of the house poised on its trembling surface. The doorbell sounded again. "All right, all right," she muttered, "I'm coming."

A girl with dark circles round her eyes stood on the doorstep. She looked vaguely familiar, and for a moment Muriel thought she recognized her from a TV

1 **hiss:** Zischen; Rauschen.
2 **sizzle:** Zischen.
5 **to grit one's teeth:** die Zähne zusammenbeißen.
6 **lingering:** anhaltend, andauernd.
7 **to slosh:** platschen, durchs schwappende Wasser waten.
9 **soaked through:** durchnässt, tropfnass.
10 **runoff:** Abfluss, abfließendes Wasser.
12 **to miscalculate:** falsch berechnen.
13 **baseboard:** Fußleiste.
16 **to hold s.th. poised:** etwas balancieren.
leaking: leck.
18 **to mutter:** murmeln.

program about a streetwalker who rises up to kill her pimp and liberate all the other leather-clad, black-eyed streetwalkers of the neighborhood, but then the girl spoke and Muriel realized her mistake. “Hi”, the girl said, and Muriel saw that her shoes were black with mud, “I’m your neighbor? Meg Terwilliger?”

Muriel was listening to the bathroom sink. She said nothing. The girl looked down at her muddy shoes. “I, uh, just wanted to tell you that we’re, uh – Sonny and I, I mean – he’s my husband? – we’re sorry about your trouble and all, but I wondered if you knew your sprinklers were on out back?”

Muriel attempted a smile – surely a smile was appropriate at this juncture, wasn’t it? – but managed only to lift her upper lip back from her teeth in a sort of wince or grimace.

The girl was noticing the rug now, and Muriel’s sodden slippers. She looked baffled, perhaps even a little frightened. And young. So young. Muriel had had a young friend once, a girl from the community college who used to come to the house before Monty got sick. She had a tape recorder, and she would ask

1 **streetwalker:** Prostituierte.
2 **pimp:** Zuhälter.
to liberate: befreien, erlösen.
14 **at this juncture:** zu diesem Zeitpunkt.
16 **wince:** Zusammenzucken.
18 **slippers:** Pantoffeln.
to look baffled: verwirrt wirken.
20f. **community college:** berufsbildende Einrichtung in den städtischen Zentren der USA mit einer Vielzahl von praktischen Kursen für die Allgemeinheit.

them questions about their childhood, about the days when the San Fernando Valley was dirt roads and orange groves. Oral history, she called it. "It's all right," Muriel said, trying to reassure her.

"I just – is it a plumbing problem?" the girl said, backing away from the door. "Sonny ..." she said, but didn't finish the thought. She ducked her head and retreated down the steps, but when she reached the walk she wheeled around. "I mean you really ought to see about the sprinklers," she blurted, "the whole place is soaked, my sunroom and everything –"

"It's all right," Muriel repeated, and then the girl was gone and she shut the door.

"She's nuts, she is. Really. I mean she's out of her gourd."

Meg was searing chunks of thresher shark in a pan with green chilies, sweet red pepper, onion, and cilantro. Sonny, who was twenty-eight and so intoxicated

2 **San Fernando Valley:** Siedlung im Nordosten von Los Angeles mit Mittelklassehäusern, die in den frühen 1970er-Jahren entstanden sind.
dirt road: unbefestigte Straße.
3 **grove:** Hain, Wäldchen.
4 **to reassure s.o.:** jdn. beruhigen.
5 **plumbing problem:** Problem mit den Wasserleitungen.
10 **to blurt:** (mit etwas) herausplatzen.
14 **nuts** (coll.): verrückt.
14f. **to be out of one's gourd** (coll.): nicht mehr alle Tassen im Schrank haben.
16 **to sear:** rasch anbraten.
chunk: Stück, Scheibe.
18 **intoxicated** (fig.): berauscht.

by real estate he had to forgo the morning paper till he got home at night, was slumped in the breakfast nook with a vodka tonic and the sports pages. His white-blond hair was cut fashionably, in what might once have been called a flattop, though it was thinning, and his open, appealing face, with its boyish look, had begun to show signs of wear, particularly around the eyes, where years of escrow had taken their toll. Tiffany was in her room, playing quietly with a pair of six-inch dolls that had cost sixty-five dollars each.

"Who?" Sonny murmured, tugging unconsciously at the gold chain he wore around his neck.

"Muriel. The old lady next door. Haven't you heard a thing I've been saying?" With an angry snap of her wrist, Meg cut the heat beneath the saucepan and clapped a lid over it. "The floor in the sunroom is flooded, for god's sake," she said, stalking across the kitchen in her bare feet till she stood poised over him. "The rug is ruined. Or almost is. And the yard –"

Sonny slapped the paper down on the table. "All right! Just let me relax a minute, will you?"

She put on her pleading look. It was a look com-

1 **real estate:** Immobilien.
to forgo s.th.: auf etwas verzichten.
2 **slumped:** zusammengesunken.
3 **nook:** Nische, Eckchen.
5 **flattop** (coll.): Bürstenhaarschnitt.
8 **escrow:** Verantwortung für Anderkonten, Treuhandverwaltung.
8f. **to take one's toll:** seinen, ihren Tribut fordern.
18 **to stalk:** pirschen.
19 **poised:** unbeweglich, schwebend.

pounded of pouty lips, tousled hair, and those inevitable eyes, and it always had its effect on him. "One minute," she murmured. "That's all it'll take. I just want you to see the backyard."

She took him by the hand and led him through the living room to the sunroom, where he stood a moment contemplating the damp spot on the concrete floor. She was surprised herself at how the spot had grown – it was three times what it had been that afternoon, and it seemed to have sprouted wings and legs like an enormous Rorschach. She pictured a butterfly. Or no, a hovering crow or bat. She wondered what Muriel would have made of it.

Outside, she let out a little yelp of disgust – all the earthworms in the yard had crawled up on the step to die. And the lawn wasn't merely spongy now, it was soaked through, puddled like a swamp. "Jesus Christ," Sonny muttered, sinking in his wingtips. He

1 **pouty** (coll.): schmollend.
tousled: zerzaust.
1 f. **inevitable:** unausweichlich.
7 **to contemplate:** betrachten.
10 **to sprout:** wachsen, sprießen.
11 **Rorschach:** nach Hermann Rorschach (1884–1922) benannter psychologischer Persönlichkeitstest mit Tintenklecksbildern.
12 **to hover:** schweben.
bat: Fledermaus.
14 **yelp:** Aufschrei.
disgust: Ekel.
15 **earthworm:** Regenwurm.
17 **puddled:** mit Pfützen übersät.
swamp: Sumpf.
18 **wingtips:** Herrenhalbschuhe mit Oberlederverzierungen.

cakewalked across the yard to where the fence had begun to sag, the post leaning drunkenly, the slats bowed. "Will you look at this?" he shouted over his shoulder. Squeamish about the worms, Meg stood at the door to the sunroom. "The goddam fence is falling down!"

He stood there a moment, water seeping into his shoes, a look of stupefaction on his face. Meg recognized the look. It stole over his features in moments of extremity, as when he tore open the phone bill to discover mysterious twenty-dollar calls to Billings, Montana, and Greenleaf, Mississippi, or when his buyer called on the day escrow was to close to tell him he'd assaulted the seller and wondered if Sonny had five hundred dollars for bail. These occasions always took him by surprise. He was shocked anew each time the crisply surveyed, neatly kept world he so cherished rose up to confront him with all its essential sloppiness, irrationality, and bad business

1 **to cakewalk:** mit staksenden Bewegungen laufen.
2 **to sag:** absacken.
slat: Latte.
4 **squeamish:** empfindlich, zimperlich.
5 **goddam** (coll.): verdammt.
7 **to seep:** sickern.
8 **stupefaction:** Verblüffung, Bestürzung.
10 **extremity:** äußerste Not, äußerste Verzweiflung.
12 **Montana:** Bundesstaat im zentralen Norden der USA.
Mississippi: Bundesstaat im Süden der USA.
14 **to assault:** angreifen.
15 **bail:** Kaution.
17 **crisply surveyed:** genauestens vermessen.
19 **sloppiness:** Schlampigkeit, Nachlässigkeit.

sense. Meg watched the look of disbelief turn to one of injured rage. She followed him through the house, up the walk, and into Muriel's yard, where he stalked up to the front door and pounded like the Gestapo. There was no response.

"Son of a bitch," he spat, turning to glare over his shoulder at her as if it were her fault or something. From inside they could hear the drama of running water, a drip and gurgle, a sough and hiss. Sonny turned back to the door, hammering his fist against it till Meg swore she could see the panels jump.

It frightened her, this sudden rage. Sure, there was a problem here and she was glad he was taking care of it, but did he have to get violent, did he have to get crazy? "You don't have to beat her door down," she called, focusing on the swell of his shoulder and the hammer of his fist as it rose and fell in savage rhythm. "Sonny, come on. It's only water, for god's sake."

"Only?" he snarled, spinning round to face her. "You saw the fence – next thing you know the foundation'll shift on us. The whole damn house –" He never finished. The look on her face told him that Muriel had opened the door.

Muriel was wearing the same faded blue housecoat

4 **to pound:** heftig klopfen, hämmern.
6 **son of a bitch** (vulg.): Miststück.
6f. **to glare at s.o.:** jdn. zornig anstarren.
9 **sough:** Rauschen.
16 **the swell of his shoulder:** der Teil seiner Schulter, der nun hochgezogen ist.
19 **to snarl:** fauchen.
24 **housecoat:** Morgenmantel.

she'd had on earlier, and the same wet slippers. Short, heavyset, so big in front it seemed as if she were about to topple over, she clung to the doorframe and peered up at Sonny out of a stony face. Meg watched as Sonny jerked round to confront her and then stopped cold when he got a look at the interior of the house. The plaster walls were stained now, drinking up the wet in long jagged fingers that clawed toward the ceiling, and a dribble of coffee-colored liquid began to seep across the doorstep and puddle at Sonny's feet. The sound of rushing water was unmistakable, even from where Meg was standing. "Yes?" Muriel said, the voice withered in her throat. "Can I help you?"

It took Sonny a minute – Meg could see it in his eyes: this was more than he could handle, willful destruction of a domicile, every tap in the place on full, the floors warped, plaster ruined – but then he recovered himself. "The water," he said. "You – our fence – I mean you can't, you've got to stop this –"

The old woman drew herself up, clutching the belt of her housedress till her knuckles bulged with the

2 **heavyset:** stark gebaut.
3 **to topple over:** umkippen.
7 **plaster:** (Wand-)Putz.
8 **jagged:** gezackt, spitz.
13 **to wither:** welken, dahinschwinden.
17 **domicile:** Domizil, Wohnsitz.
18 **to warp:** sich verbiegen, verziehen, wellen.
22 **to clutch:** umklammert halten.
23 **to bulge:** sich wölben, hervortreten.

tension. She looked first at Meg, still planted in the corner of the yard, and then turned to Sonny. "Water?" she said. "What water?"

The young man at the door reminded her, in a way, of Monty. Something about the eyes or the set of the ears – or maybe it was the crisp high cut of the side-burns … Of course, most young men reminded her of Monty. The Monty of fifty years ago, that is. The Monty who'd opened up the world to her over the shift lever of his Model-A Ford, not the crabbed and abrasive old man who called her bonehead and dildo and cuffed her like a dog. Monty. When the stroke brought him down, she was almost glad. She saw him pinned beneath his tubes in the hospital and something stirred in her; she brought him home and changed his bedpan, peered into the vaults of his eyes, fed him Gerber's like the baby she'd never had, and she knew it was over. Fifty years. No more drunken rages, no more pans flung against the wall, never again his sour flesh pressed to hers. She was on top now.

6 f. **sideburns:** Koteletten.
10 **shift lever:** Schalthebel.
Model-A Ford: Der erste Model-A-Ford lief 1927 vom Band und wurde bis 1932 produziert.
crabbed: griesgrämig, mürrisch.
11 **abrasive:** aggressiv.
bonehead (coll.): Dummkopf.
dildo: Dildo, Vibrator (Sexspielzeug).
12 **to cuff s.o.:** jdm. einen Klaps geben.
16 **vault:** Höhle.
17 **Gerber's:** Handelsname einer bekannten Babynahrung.

The second young man – he was a Mexican, short, stocky, with a mustache so thin it could have been penciled on and wicked little red-flecked eyes – also reminded her of Monty. Not so much in the way he looked as in the way he held himself, the way he swaggered and puffed out his chest. And the uniform too, of course. Monty had worn a uniform during the war.

"Mrs. Burgess?" the Mexican asked.

Muriel stood at the open door. It was dusk, the heat cut as if there were a thermostat in the sky. She'd been sitting in the dark. The electricity had gone out on her – something to do with the water and the wires. She nodded her head in response to the policeman's question.

"We've had a complaint," he said.

Little piggy eyes. A complaint. *We've had a complaint.* He wasn't fooling her, not for a minute. She knew what they wanted, the police, the girl next door, and the boy she was married to – they wanted to bring Monty back. Prop him up against the bedframe, stick his legs back under him, put the bellow back in his voice. Oh, no, they weren't fooling her.

She followed the policeman around the darkened house as he went from faucet to faucet, sink to tub to

2 **stocky:** stämmig.
mustache: Schnurrbart.
5 **in the way he held himself:** in seiner Körperhaltung.
6 **to swagger:** stolzieren.
10 **dusk:** Abenddämmerung.
21 **to prop:** stützen, lehnen.
22 **bellow:** Brüllen.

shower. He firmly twisted each of the taps closed and drained the basins, then crossed the patio to kill the sprinklers and the hose too. "Are you all right?" he kept asking. "Are you all right?"

She had to hold her chin in her palm to keep her lips from trembling. "If you mean am I in possession of my faculties, yes, I am, thank you. I am all right."

They were back at the front door now. He leaned nonchalantly against the doorframe and dropped his voice to a confidential whisper. "So what's this with the water then?"

She wouldn't answer him. She knew her rights. What business was it of his, or anybody's, what she did with her own taps and her own sprinklers? She could pay the water bill. Had paid it, in fact. Eleven hundred dollars' worth. She watched his eyes and shrugged.

"Next of kin?" he asked. "Daughter? Son? Anybody we can call?"

Now her lips held. She shook her head.

He gave it a moment, then let out a sigh. "Okay," he said, speaking slowly and with exaggerated emphasis, as if he were talking to a child, "I'm going now. You leave the water alone – wash your face, brush your teeth, do the dishes. But no more of this." He swaggered back from her, fingering his belt, his

2 **to kill:** ausschalten, abdrehen.
7 **faculties:** geistige Kräfte.
9 **nonchalantly** (adv.): lässig.
10 **confidential:** vertraulich.
17 **to shrug:** die Achseln zucken.
18 **next of kin:** nächste(r) Angehörige(r).

holster, the dead weight of his nightstick. "One more complaint and we'll have to take you into custody for your own good. You're endangering yourself and the neighbors too. Understand?"

Smile, she told herself, smile. "Oh, yes," she said softly. "Yes, I understand."

He held her eyes a moment, threatening her – just like Monty used to do, just like Monty – and then he was gone.

She stood there on the doorstep a long while, the night deepening around her. She listened to the cowbirds, the wild parakeets that nested in the Murtaughs' palm, the whoosh of traffic from the distant freeway. After a while, she sat on the step. Behind her, the house was silent: no faucet dripped, no sprinkler hissed, no toilet gurgled. It was horrible. Insupportable. In the pit of that dry silence she could hear him, Monty, treading the buckled floors, pouring himself another vodka, cursing her in a voice like sandpaper.

She couldn't go back in there. Not tonight. The place was deadly, contaminated, sick as the grave –

1 **holster:** (Pistolen-)Halfter.
nightstick: Schlagstock.
2 **to take s.o. into custody:** jdn. in Gewahrsam nehmen, verhaften.
11 f. **cowbird:** Kuhstärling (amerikanischer Singvogel, der Ungeziefer aus dem Fell von weidendem Vieh aufpickt).
12 **parakeet:** Sittich.
13 **whoosh:** Rauschen.
14 **freeway:** Autobahn.
18 **buckled:** verbogen, verzogen, gewellt.
22 **contaminated:** verseucht, verunreinigt.

after all was said and done, it just wasn't clean enough. If the rest of it was a mystery – oral history, fifty years of Monty, the girl with the blackened eyes – that much she understood.

Meg was watering the cane plant in the living room when the police cruiser came for the old lady next door. The police had been there the night before and Sonny had stood out front with his arms folded while the officer shut down Muriel's taps and sprinklers. "I guess that's that," he said, coming up the walk in the oversized Hawaiian shirt she'd given him for Father's Day. But in the morning, the sprinklers were on again and Sonny called the local substation three times before he left for work. She's crazy, he'd hollered into the phone, irresponsible, a threat to herself and the community. He had a four-year-old daughter to worry about, for christ's sake. A dog. A wife. His fence was falling down. Did they have any idea what that amount of water was going to do to the substrata beneath the house?

Now the police were back. The patrol car stretched across the window and slid silently into the driveway next door. Meg set down the watering can. She was wearing her Fila sweats and a new pair of Nikes and her hair was tied back in a red scarf. She'd dropped Tiffany off at nursery school, but she had the water-

5 **cane: 1.** Zuckerrohr; **2.** im Süden der USA heimisches hohes Ziergras.
14 **to holler** (coll.): brüllen.
19 **substratum** (pl. *substrata*): untere Erdschicht.

ing and her stretching exercises to do and a pasta salad to make before she picked up Queenie at the vet's. Still, she went directly to the front door and then out onto the walk.

The police – it took her a minute to realize that the shorter of the two was a woman – were on Muriel's front porch, looking stiff and uncertain in their razor-creased uniforms. The man knocked first – once, twice, three times. Nothing happened. Then the woman knocked. Still nothing. Meg folded her arms and waited. After a minute, the man went around to the side gate and let himself into the yard. Meg heard the sprinklers die with a wheeze, and then the officer was back, his shoes heavy with mud.

Again he thumped at the door, much more violently now, and Meg thought of Sonny. "Open up," the woman called in a breathy contralto she tried unsuccessfully to deepen, "police."

It was then that Meg saw her, Muriel, at the bay window on the near side of the door. "Look," she shouted before she knew what she was saying, "she's there, there in the window!"

The male officer – he had a mustache and pale, fine hair like Sonny's – leaned out over the railing and gestured impatiently at the figure behind the window. "Police," he growled. "Open the door." Muriel never

7 **porch:** (offene) Veranda.
7 f. **razor-creased:** mit messerscharfer Bügelfalte.
17 **breathy:** hauchig.
contralto: Altstimme.
19 f. **bay window:** Erkerfenster.
26 **to growl:** knurren.

moved. "All right," he grunted, cursing under his breath, "all right," and he put his shoulder to the door. There was nothing to it. The frame splintered, water dribbled out, and both officers disappeared into the house.

Meg waited. She had things to do, yes, but she waited anyway, bending to pull the odd dandelion the gardener had missed, trying to look busy. The police were in there an awful long time – twenty minutes, half an hour – and then the woman appeared in the doorway with Muriel.

Muriel seemed heavier than ever, her face pouchy, arms swollen. She was wearing white sandals on her old splayed feet, a shapeless print dress, and a white straw hat that looked as if it had been dug out of a box in the attic. The woman had her by the arm; the man loomed behind her with a suitcase. Down the steps and up the walk, she never turned her head. But then, just as the policewoman was helping her into the backseat of the patrol car, Muriel swung round as if to take one last look at her house. But it wasn't the house she was looking at: it was Meg.

1 **to grunt:** grunzen.
3 **there was nothing to it:** es war kinderleicht.
to splinter: (zer)splittern.
7 **dandelion:** Löwenzahn.
12 **pouchy:** aufgedunsen.
14 **splayed feet:** Spreizfüße.
16 **attic:** Mansarde, Dachboden.
17 **to loom:** aufragen.

The morning gave way to the heat of afternoon. Meg finished the watering, made the pasta salad – bow-tie twists, fresh salmon, black olives, and pine nuts – ran her errands, picked up Tiffany, and put her down for a nap. Somehow, though, she just couldn't get Muriel out of her head. The old lady had stared at her for five seconds maybe, and then the policewoman was coaxing her into the car. Meg had felt like sinking into the ground. But then she realized that Muriel's look wasn't vengeful at all – it was just sad. It was a look that said this is what it comes to. Fifty years and this is what it comes to.

The backyard was an inferno, the sun poised directly overhead. Queenie, defleaed, shampooed, and with her toenails clipped, was stretched out asleep in the shade beside the pool. It was quiet. Even the birds were still. Meg took off her Nikes and walked barefoot through the sopping grass to the fence, or what was left of it. The post had buckled overnight, canting the whole business into Muriel's yard. Meg never hesitated. She sprang up onto the plane of the slats and dropped to the grass on the other side.

Her feet sank in the mud, the earth like pudding,

2f. **bow-tie twists:** Farfalle, Schmetterlingsnudeln.
3 **pine nuts:** Pinienkerne.
3f. **to run one's errands:** Besorgungen machen.
5 **nap:** Schläfchen, Nickerchen.
8 **to coax:** locken.
10 **vengeful:** rachsüchtig.
14 **defleaed:** entfloht, von Flöhen befreit.
18 **sopping:** völlig durchnässt.
20 **to cant:** sich neigen, kippen.

like chocolate pudding, and as she lifted her feet to move toward the house the tracks she left behind her slowly filled with water. The patio was an island. She crossed it, dodging potted plants and wicker furniture, and tried the back door; finding it locked, she moved to the window, shaded her face with her hands, and peered in. The sight made her catch her breath. The plaster was crumbling, wallpaper peeling, the rug and floors ruined: she knew it was bad, but this was crazy, this was suicide.

Grief, that's what it was. Or was it? And then she was thinking of Sonny again – what if he was dead and she was old like Muriel? She wouldn't be so fat, of course, but maybe like one of those thin and elegant old ladies in Palm Springs, the ones who'd done their stretching all their lives. Or what if she wasn't an old lady at all – the thought swooped down on her like a bird out of the sky – what if Sonny was in a car wreck or something? It could happen.

She stood there gazing in on the mess through her own wavering reflection. One moment she saw the wreckage of the old lady's life, the next the fine mouth and expressive eyes everyone commented on. After a while, she turned away from the window and looked out on the yard as Muriel must have seen it. There were the roses, gorged with water and flower-

4 **wicker:** Korbgeflecht.
8 **to crumble** (ab)bröckeln.
to peel: abblättern (Tapete).
17 **to swoop down:** einen Sturzflug machen.
21 **to waver:** schwanken, flackern.

ing madly, the impatiens, rigid as sticks, oleander drowning in their own yellowed leaves – and there, poking innocuously from the bushes at the far corner of the patio, was the steel wand that controlled the sprinklers. Handle, neck, prongs: it was just like theirs.

And then it came to her. She'd turn them on – the sprinklers – just for a minute, to see what it felt like. She wouldn't leave them on long – it could threaten the whole foundation of her house.

That much she understood.

3 **innocuously** (adv.): harmlos.
4 **wand:** Stab.
5 **prong:** Zacke, Zinke.

Carnal Knowledge

I'd never really thought much about meat. It was there in the supermarket in a plastic wrapper; it came between slices of bread with mayo and mustard and a dill pickle on the side; it sputtered and smoked on the grill till somebody flipped it over, and then it appeared on the plate, between the baked potato and the julienne carrots, neatly cross-hatched and floating in a puddle of red juice. Beef, mutton, pork, venison, dripping burgers and greasy ribs – it was all the same to me, food, the body's fuel, something to savor a moment on the tongue before the digestive system went to work on it. Which is not to say I was totally unconscious of the deeper implications. Every once in a

1 **carnal:** fleischlich, sinnlich.
3 **wrapper:** Verpackung.
5 **dill pickle:** saure Gurke.
to sputter: brutzeln, zischen.
6 **to flip s.th. over:** etwas schnell umdrehen.
8 **julienne:** in schmale Streifen geschnitten.
cross-hatched: in Kreuzlage angerichtet.
9 **puddle:** Pfütze.
mutton: Hammel(fleisch).
venison: Rehfleisch.
10 **greasy:** fettig, fetttriefend.
11 **to savor:** kosten, genießen.
12 **digestive system:** Verdauungstrakt.
14 **implication:** Bedeutung.

while I'd eat at home, a quartered chicken, a package of Shake 'n Bake, Stove Top stuffing and frozen peas, and as I hacked away at the stippled yellow skin and pink flesh of the sanitized bird I'd wonder at the darkish bits of organ clinging to the ribs – what was that, liver? kidney? – but in the end it didn't make me any less fond of Kentucky Fried or Chicken McNuggets. I saw those ads in the magazines, too, the ones that showed the veal calves penned up in their own waste, their limbs atrophied and their veins so pumped full of antibiotics they couldn't control their bowels, but when I took a date to Anna Maria's, I could never resist the veal scallopini.

And then I met Alena Jorgensen.

It was a year ago, two weeks before Thanksgiving – I remember the date because it was my birthday, my thirtieth, and I'd called in sick and gone to the beach to warm my face, read a book and feel a little sorry for myself. The Santa Anas were blowing and it was

2 **Shake 'n Bake:** Handelsname einer gewürzten Panade.
Stove Top stuffing: Handelsname einer Geflügelfüllung.
3 **stippled:** pockig.
4 **sanitized:** gesäubert, gereinigt.
8 **ad:** Kurzform von *advertisement*.
9 **veal:** Kalbfleisch.
penned up: eingesperrt.
10 **atrophied:** verkümmert.
11 **bowels** (pl.): Gedärm.
12 **Anna Maria's:** bekanntes Lokal einer Gourmetköchin in San Francisco.
13 **scallopini** (Ital.): dünne Fleischscheiben.
17 **to call in sick:** sich krankmelden.
19 **Santa Anas** (pl.): trockener Wind im Spätsommer oder Herbst in Südkalifornien.

clear all the way to Catalina, but there was an edge to the air, a scent of winter hanging over Utah, and as far as I could see in either direction I had the beach pretty much to myself. I found a sheltered spot in a tumble of boulders, spread a blanket and settled down to attack the pastrami on rye I'd brought along for nourishment. Then I turned to my book – a comfortingly apocalyptic tract about the demise of the planet – and let the sun warm me as I read about the denuding of the rain forest, the poisoning of the atmosphere and the swift silent eradication of species. Gulls coasted by overhead. I saw the distant glint of jetliners.

I must have dozed, my head thrown back, the book spread open in my lap, because the next thing I remember, a strange dog was hovering over me and the sun had dipped behind the rocks. The dog was big, wild-haired, with one staring blue eye, and it just

1 **Catalina:** Ferieninsel bei Los Angeles.
1f. **there was an edge to the air:** man spürte eine Kälte in der Luft.
2 **Utah:** US-Bundesstaat.
5 **tumble of boulders:** wahllos herumliegende Felsbrocken.
6 **pastrami on rye:** geräuchertes, stark gewürztes Rindfleisch auf Roggenbrot.
7 **nourishment:** Nahrung.
8 **apocalyptic tract:** apokalyptisches Traktat.
demise: Tod, Ende.
10 **denuding:** Abholzung.
11 **eradication:** Ausrottung.
12 **gull:** Möwe.
glint: Glitzern.
14 **to doze:** dösen.
16 **to hover:** herumlungern.

looked at me, ears slightly cocked, as if it expected a Milk-Bone or something. I was startled – not that I don't like dogs, but here was this woolly thing poking its snout in my face – and I guess I must have made some sort of defensive gesture, because the dog staggered back a step and froze. Even in the confusion of the moment I could see that there was something wrong with this dog, an unsteadiness, a gimp, a wobble to its legs. I felt a mixture of pity and revulsion – had it been hit by a car, was that it? – when all at once I became aware of a wetness on the breast of my windbreaker, and an unmistakable odor rose to my nostrils: I'd been pissed on.

Pissed on. As I lay there unsuspecting, enjoying the sun, the beach, the solitude, this stupid beast had lifted its leg and used me as a pissoir – and now it was poised there on the edge of the blanket as if it expected a reward. A sudden rage seized me. I came up off the blanket with a curse, and it was only then that

1 **ears slightly cocked:** die Ohren leicht gespitzt.
2 **Milk-Bone:** Handelsname eines Hundeknochens oder -kuchens.
startled: erschrocken.
3 **to poke:** stoßen.
4 **snout:** Schnauze.
5 f. **to stagger:** torkeln.
8 **gimp:** Wanken.
wobble: Wackeln.
9 **revulsion:** Abscheu, Ekel.
11 f. **windbreaker:** Windjacke.
12 **odor:** Geruch.
12 f. **nostrils** (pl.): Nase (*nostril:* Nasenloch).
15 **solitude:** Einsamkeit.
16 f. **it was poised there:** er hatte sich (vor mir) aufgebaut.

a dim apprehension seemed to seep into the dog's other eye, the brown one, and it lurched back and fell on its face, just out of reach. And then it lurched and fell again, bobbing and weaving across the sand like a seal out of water. I was on my feet now, murderous, glad to see that the thing was hobbled – it would simplify the task of running it down and beating it to death.

"Alf!" a voice called, and as the dog floundered in the sand, I turned and saw Alena Jorgensen poised on the boulder behind me. I don't want to make too much of the moment, don't want to mythologize it or clutter the scene with allusions to Aphrodite rising from the waves or accepting the golden apple from Paris, but she was a pretty impressive sight. Barelegged, fluid, as tall and uncompromising as her Nordic ancestors and dressed in a Gore-Tex bikini and hooded sweatshirt unzipped to the waist, she blew me

1 **to seep into s.th.:** in etwas hineinsickern.
2 **to lurch:** sich ruckartig bewegen.
4 **to bob:** sich auf und ab bewegen.
to weave: sich winden.
6 **to be hobbled:** hinken.
9 **to flounder:** sich abzappeln.
13 **to clutter:** voll stopfen; hier: (fig.) überfrachten.
Aphrodite: griechische Göttin der Liebe und Schönheit.
15 **Paris:** schöner Sohn des mythischen Königs Priamos von Troja; entschied einen Streit zugunsten Aphrodites.
16 **fluid** (fig.): geschmeidig.
uncompromising: kompromisslos.
17 **ancestor:** Vorfahr.
18 **hooded:** mit Kapuze.
18 f. **she blew me away** (fig.): sie haute mich um.

away, in any event. Piss-spattered and stupefied, I could only gape up at her.

"You bad boy," she said, scolding, "you get out of there." She glanced from the dog to me and back again. "Oh, you bad boy, what have you done?" she demanded, and I was ready to admit to anything, but it was the dog she was addressing, and the dog flopped over in the sand as if it had been shot. Alena skipped lightly down from the rock, and in the next moment, before I could protest, she was rubbing at the stain on my windbreaker with the wadded-up hem of her sweatshirt.

I tried to stop her – "It's all right," I said, "it's nothing," as if dogs routinely pissed on my wardrobe – but she wouldn't hear of it.

"No," she said, rubbing, her hair flying in my face, the naked skin of her thigh pressed unconsciously to my own, "no, this is terrible, I'm so embarrassed – Alf, you bad boy – I'll clean it for you, I will, it's the least – oh, look at that, it's stained right through to your T-shirt –"

I could smell her, the mousse she used in her hair, a lilac soap or perfume, the salt-sweet odor of her sweat

1 **stupefied:** benommen.
2 **to gape up at s.o.:** jdn. mit offenem Mund anstarren.
3 **to scold:** schelten.
8 **to flop over:** sich fallen lassen, hinplumpsen.
11 **wadded-up:** zusammengeknüllt.
hem: Saum.
17 **thigh:** (Ober-)Schenkel.
unconsciously (adv.): unbeabsichtigt.
22 **mousse:** Haarspray, Festiger.
23 **lilac:** Flieder.

– she'd been jogging, that was it. I murmured something about taking it to the cleaner's myself.

She stopped rubbing and straightened up. She was my height, maybe even a fraction taller, and her eyes were ever so slightly mismatched, like the dog's: a deep earnest blue in the right iris, shading to sea-green and turquoise in the left. We were so close we might have been dancing. "Tell you what," she said, and her face lit with a smile, "since you're so nice about the whole thing, and most people wouldn't be, even if they knew what poor Alf has been through, why don't you let me wash it for you – and the T-shirt too?"

I was a little disconcerted at this point – I was the one who'd been pissed on, after all – but my anger was gone. I felt weightless, adrift, like a piece of fluff floating on the breeze. "Listen," I said, and for the moment I couldn't look her in the eye, "I don't want to put you to any trouble. ..."

"I'm ten minutes up the beach, and I've got a washer and dryer. Come on, it's no trouble at all. Or do you have plans? I mean, I could just pay for the cleaner's if you want. ..."

I was between relationships – the person I'd been seeing off and on for the past year wouldn't even return my calls – and my plans consisted of taking in a solitary late-afternoon movie as a birthday treat, then

4 **a fraction taller:** eine Spur größer.
13 **disconcerted:** beunruhigt.
15 **adrift:** durcheinander, losgelöst.
fluff: Fusseln.
26 **solitary:** einsam.
treat: besonderes Vergnügen, Geschenk.

heading over to my mother's for dinner and the cake with the candles. My Aunt Irene would be there, and so would my grandmother. They would exclaim over how big I was and how handsome and then they would begin to contrast my present self with my previous, more diminutive incarnations, and finally work themselves up to a spate of reminiscence that would continue unabated till my mother drove them home. And then, if I was lucky, I'd go out to a singles bar and make the acquaintance of a divorced computer programmer in her mid-thirties with three kids and bad breath.

I shrugged. "Plans? No, not really. I mean, nothing in particular."

Alena was housesitting a one-room bungalow that rose stumplike from the sand, no more than fifty feet from the tide line. There were trees in the yard behind it and the place was sandwiched between glass fortresses with crenellated decks, whipping flags and great hulking concrete pylons. Sitting on the couch in-

6 **diminutive:** klein, unwichtig.
7 **a spate of reminiscence:** eine Flut von Erinnerungen.
8 **unabated:** ungehindert.
13 **to shrug:** die Achseln zucken.
15 **to housesit:** das Haus hüten.
16 **stumplike:** wie ein Baumstumpf.
18f. **fortress:** Festung.
19 **crenellated:** mit Zinnen versehen.
deck: Sonnenterrasse.
whipping: flatternd.
20 **hulking:** massig.
pylon: Mast.

side, you could feel the dull reverberation of each wave hitting the shore, a slow steady pulse that forever defined the place for me. Alena gave me a faded UC Davis sweatshirt that nearly fit, sprayed a stain remover on my T-shirt and windbreaker, and in a single fluid motion flipped down the lid of the washer and extracted two beers from the refrigerator beside it.

There was an awkward moment as she settled into the chair opposite me and we concentrated on our beers. I didn't know what to say. I was disoriented, giddy, still struggling to grasp what had happened. Fifteen minutes earlier I'd been dozing on the beach, alone on my birthday and feeling sorry for myself, and now I was ensconced in a cozy beach house, in the presence of Alena Jorgensen and her naked spill of leg, drinking a beer. "So what do you do?" she said, setting her beer down on the coffee table.

I was grateful for the question, too grateful maybe. I described to her at length how dull my job was, nearly ten years with the same agency, writing ad copy, my brain gone numb with disuse. I was somewhere in the middle of a blow-by-blow account of our current campaign for a Ghanian vodka distilled from

1 **reverberation:** Widerhall.
3f. **UC Davis:** Universität in Kalifornien.
11 **giddy:** schwindlig.
to grasp: begreifen.
14 **I was ensconced:** ich hatte mich niedergelassen.
15f. **her naked spill of leg:** etwa: ihre überwältigenden nackten Beine.
19 **at length:** ausführlich.
20f. **ad copy:** Werbetexte.
21 **numb:** wie betäubt.
22 **blow-by-blow account:** detaillierter Bericht.

calabash husks when she said, "I know what you mean," and told me she'd dropped out of veterinary school herself. "After I saw what they did to the animals. I mean, can you see neutering a dog just for our convenience, just because it's easier for us if they don't have a sex life?" Her voice grew hot. "It's the same old story, species fascism at its worst."

Alf was lying at my feet, grunting softly and looking up mournfully out of his staring blue eye, as blameless a creature as ever lived. I made a small noise of agreement and then focused on Alf. "And your dog," I said, "he's arthritic? Or is it hip dysplasia or what?" I was pleased with myself for the question – aside from "tapeworm," "hip dysplasia" was the only veterinary term I could dredge up from the memory bank, and I could see that Alf's problems ran deeper than worms.

Alena looked angry suddenly. "Don't I wish," she said. She paused to draw a bitter breath. "There's nothing wrong with Alf that wasn't inflicted on him. They tortured him, maimed him, mutilated him."

1 **calabash husk:** Kalebassen-, Flaschenkürbisschale.
4 **to neuter:** kastrieren.
7 **species fascism:** Artenfaschismus.
8 **to grunt:** grunzen.
9 **mournfully** (adv.): traurig.
12 **hip dysplasia:** Hüftdysplasie, Fehl-, Unterentwicklung der Hüfte.
14 **tapeworm:** Bandwurm.
15 **to dredge s.th. up:** (fig.) etwas hervorkramen.
18 **don't I wish** (coll.): schön wär's.
20 **to inflict s.th. on s.o.:** jdm. etwas zufügen.
21 **to maim:** zum Krüppel machen.
to mutilate: verstümmeln.

"Tortured him?" I echoed, feeling the indignation rise in me – this beautiful girl, this innocent beast. "Who?"

Alena leaned forward and there was real hate in her eyes. She mentioned a prominent shoe company – spat out the name, actually. It was an ordinary name, a familiar one, and it hung in the air between us, suddenly sinister. Alf had been part of an experiment to market booties for dogs – suede, cordovan, patent leather, the works. The dogs were made to pace a treadmill in their booties, to assess wear; Alf was part of the control group.

"Control group?" I could feel the hackles rising on the back of my neck.

"They used eighty-grit sandpaper on the treads, to accelerate the process." Alena shot a glance out the window to where the surf pounded the shore; she bit her lip. "Alf was one of the dogs without booties."

I was stunned. I wanted to get up and comfort her,

1 **indignation:** Entrüstung.
8 **sinister:** unheimlich, finster.
9 **booty:** Stiefelette.
suede: Wildleder.
cordovan: weiches Leder.
9f. **patent leather:** Lackleder.
10 **the works** (coll.): alles Drum und Dran.
10f. **to pace a treadmill:** auf einem Laufband gehen.
11 **to assess:** beurteilen.
13 **I could feel the hackles rising** (coll.): ich spürte, wie sich alles in mir sträubte (*hackles:* Nackenhaare).
15 **eighty-grit sandpaper:** Sandpapier mit 80er-Körnung.
17 **to pound s.th.:** gegen etwas schlagen.
19 **stunned:** wie betäubt.

but I might as well have been grafted to the chair. "I don't believe it," I said. "How could anybody –"

"Believe it," she said. She studied me a moment, then set down her beer and crossed the room to dig through a cardboard box in the corner. If I was moved by the emotion she'd called up, I was moved even more by the sight of her bending over the box in her Gore-Tex bikini; I clung to the edge of the chair as if it were a plunging roller coaster. A moment later she dropped a dozen file folders in my lap. The uppermost bore the name of the shoe company, and it was crammed with news clippings, several pages of a diary relating to plant operations and workers' shifts at the Grand Rapids facility and a floor plan of the laboratories. The folders beneath it were inscribed with the names of cosmetics firms, biomedical research centers, furriers, tanners, meatpackers. Alena perched on the edge of the coffee table and watched as I shuffled through them.

1 **grafted:** aufgepfropft.
9 **to plunge:** hinabstürzen, in die Tiefe sausen.
roller coaster: Achterbahn.
10 **file folder:** Aktenmappe.
12 **crammed:** voll gestopft.
news clippings: Zeitungsausschnitte.
14 **Grand Rapids:** Stadt im Bundesstaat Michigan.
15 **inscribed:** beschrieben.
17 **furrier:** Kürschner(in).
tanner: Gerber(in).
to perch: hocken, hoch sitzen.
19 **to shuffle through s.th.:** etwas rasch durchblättern; etwas durcheinander bringen.

"You know the Draize test?"

I gave her a blank look.

"They inject chemicals into rabbits' eyes to see how much it'll take before they go blind. The rabbits are in cages, thousands of them, and they take a needle and jab it into their eyes – and you know why, you know in the name of what great humanitarian cause this is going on, even as we speak?"

I didn't know. The surf pounded at my feet. I glanced at Alf and then back into her angry eyes.

"Mascara, that's what. Mascara. They torture countless thousands of rabbits so women can look like sluts."

I thought the characterization a bit harsh, but when I studied her pale lashes and tight lipstickless mouth, I saw that she meant it. At any rate, the notion set her off, and she launched into a two-hour lecture, gesturing with her flawless hands, quoting figures, digging through her files for the odd photo of legless mice or morphine-addicted gerbils. She told me how she'd rescued Alf herself, raiding the laboratory with six other members of the Animal Liberation Front, the

1 **Draize test:** Schleimhautverträglichkeitstest an Kaninchen.
6 **to jab:** stoßen, stechen.
13 **slut** (coll.): Schlampe.
15 **lash:** Wimper.
16 **notion:** Gedanke, Vorstellung.
16f. **to set s.o. off:** jdn. in Fahrt bringen.
17 **to launch into s.th.:** mit etwas loslegen.
18 **flawless:** makellos.
20 **gerbil:** Wüstenspringmaus.
22 **Animal Liberation Front:** radikale Tierschutzorganisation.

militant group in honor of which Alf had been named. At first, she'd been content to write letters and carry placards, but now, with the lives of so many animals at stake, she'd turned to more direct action: harassment, vandalism, sabotage. She described how she'd spiked trees with Earth-First!-ers in Oregon, cut miles of barbed-wire fence on cattle ranches in Nevada, destroyed records in biomedical research labs up and down the coast and insinuated herself between the hunters and the bighorn sheep in the mountains of Arizona. I could only nod and exclaim, smile ruefully and whistle in a low "holy cow!" sort of way. Finally, she paused to level her unsettling eyes on me. "You know what Isaac Bashevis Singer said?"

We were on our third beer. The sun was gone. I didn't have a clue.

Alena leaned forward. "'Every day is Auschwitz for the animals.'"

3 **placard:** Transparent.
4 *(to be)* **at stake:** auf dem Spiel stehen.
5 **harassment:** Belästigung.
6 **to spike trees:** Bäume mit Stahlnägeln spicken.
Earth-First!-er: Mitglied der radikalen Umweltschutzorganisation Earth-First!
7 **barbed wire fence:** Stacheldrahtzaun.
9 **to insinuate o.s. between s.o.:** sich bei jdm. einschleichen.
10 **bighorn sheep:** Dickhornschaf (Wildschaf im westlichen Nordamerika).
11 **to nod:** nicken.
11 f. **ruefully** (adv.): reuevoll.
12 **holy cow!** (coll.): heiliger Bimbam!
13 **unsettling:** verwirrend, verstörend.
14 **Singer:** Isaac Beshevis S. (1904–91), amerikanischer Schriftsteller und Philosoph polnisch-jüdischer Herkunft.

I looked down into the amber aperture of my beer bottle and nodded my head sadly. The dryer had stopped an hour and a half ago. I wondered if she'd go out to dinner with me, and what she could eat if she did. "Uh, I was wondering," I said, "if … if you might want to go out for something to eat –"

Alf chose that moment to heave himself up from the floor and urinate on the wall behind me. My dinner proposal hung in the balance as Alena shot up off the edge of the table to scold him and then gently usher him out the door. "Poor Alf," she sighed, turning back to me with a shrug. "But listen, I'm sorry if I talked your head off – I didn't mean to, but it's rare to find somebody on your own wavelength."

She smiled. *On your own wavelength:* the words illuminated me, excited me, sent up a tremor I could feel all the way down in the deepest nodes of my reproductive tract. "So how about dinner?" I persisted. Restaurants were running through my head – would it have to be veggie? Could there be even a whiff of

1 **amber:** bernsteinfarben.
aperture: Öffnung.
7 **to heave o.s. up:** sich hochwuchten.
11 **to usher:** führen, geleiten.
12 **shrug:** Achselzucken.
13 **to talk s.o.'s head off:** jdn. vollquasseln.
15 f. **to illuminate s.o.:** jdn. erleuchten.
16 **tremor:** Zittern, Beben.
17 f. **the deepest nodes of my reproductive tract:** die tiefsten Knoten meines Fortpflanzungstraktes.
18 **to persist:** beharrlich bleiben, nicht nachgeben.
20 **whiff:** Hauch.

grilled flesh on the air? Curdled goat's milk and tabbouleh, tofu, lentil soup, sprouts: *Every day is Auschwitz for the animals.* "No place with meat, of course."

She just looked at me.

"I mean, I don't eat meat myself," I lied, "or actually, not anymore" – since the pastrami sandwich, that is – "but I don't really know any place that ..." I trailed off lamely.

"I'm a Vegan," she said.

After two hours of blind bunnies, butchered calves and mutilated pups, I couldn't resist the joke. "I'm from Venus myself."

She laughed, but I could see she didn't find it all that funny. Vegans didn't eat meat or fish, she explained, or milk or cheese or eggs, and they didn't wear wool or leather – or fur, of course.

"Of course," I said. We were both standing there, hovering over the coffee table. I was beginning to feel a little foolish.

"Why don't we just eat here," she said.

The deep throb of the ocean seemed to settle in my bones as we lay there in bed that night, Alena and I, and I learned all about the fluency of her limbs and

1 **curdled:** geronnen.
1 f. **tabbouleh:** libanesischer Salat aus Couscous, Tomaten, Petersilie, Minze, Zwiebeln, Zitronensaft und Olivenöl.
2 **lentil:** Linse.
8 **to trail off:** verstummen.
11 **pup:** Welpe.
18 **to hover:** wartend, zögernd herumstehen, sich herumdrücken.
21 **throb:** Dröhnen.
23 **fluency:** Geschmeidigkeit.

the sweetness of her vegetable tongue. Alf sprawled on the floor beneath us, wheezing and groaning in his sleep, and I blessed him for his incontinence and his doggy stupidity. Something was happening to me – I could feel it in the way the boards shifted under me, feel it with each beat of the surf – and I was ready to go along with it. In the morning, I called in sick again.

Alena was watching me from bed as I dialed the office and described how the flu had migrated from my head to my gut and beyond, and there was a look in her eye that told me I would spend the rest of the day right there beside her, peeling grapes and dropping them one by one between her parted and expectant lips. I was wrong. Half an hour later, after a breakfast of brewer's yeast and what appeared to be some sort of bark marinated in yogurt, I found myself marching up and down the sidewalk in front of a fur emporium in Beverly Hills, waving a placard that read HOW DOES IT FEEL TO WEAR A CORPSE? in letters that dripped like blood.

It was a shock. I'd seen protest marches on TV, antiwar rallies and civil-rights demonstrations and all

1 **to sprawl:** ausgestreckt liegen.
2 **to wheeze:** keuchen.
9 **to migrate:** wandern, überwechseln.
10 **gut:** Bauch.
15 **brewer's yeast:** Bierhefe.
17 **emporium:** Warenhaus.
19 **corpse:** Leiche.
22 **antiwar rally:** Kundgebung gegen den Krieg, Friedenskundgebung.
civil-rights demonstration: Bürgerrechtsdemonstration.

that, but I'd never warmed my heels on the pavement or chanted slogans or felt the naked stick in my hand. There were maybe forty of us in all, mostly women, and we waved our placards at passing cars and blocked traffic on the sidewalk. One woman had smeared her face and hands with cold cream steeped in red dye, and Alena had found a ratty mink stole somewhere – the kind that features whole animals sewed together, snout to tail, their miniature limbs dangling – and she'd taken a can of crimson spray paint to their muzzles so that they looked freshly killed. She brandished this grisly banner on a stick high above her head, whooping like a savage and chanting, "Fur is death, fur is death," over and over again till it became a mantra for the crowd. The day was unseasonably warm, the Jaguars glinted in the sun and the palms nodded in the breeze, and no one, but for a single tightlipped salesman glowering from behind

1 **I'd never warmed my heels on the pavement** (fig.): ich hatte mich nie selbst beteiligt.
2 **to chant:** skandieren.
6 **to smear:** beschmieren.
6f. **cold cream steeped in red dye:** rot gefärbte Feuchtigkeitscreme, (*to steep:* tauchen, einweichen, baden).
7 **ratty:** verlottert.
mink stole: Nerzstola.
10 **to dangle:** herabhängen, baumeln.
11 **muzzle:** Maul.
12 **to brandish:** schwingen, schwenken.
grisly: grausig.
13 **to whoop like a savage:** wie eine Wilde schreien.
15f. **unseasonably** (adv.): übermäßig.
18 **to glower:** ein finsteres Gesicht machen.

the store's immaculate windows, paid the slightest bit of attention to us.

I marched out there on the street, feeling exposed and conspicuous, but marching nonetheless – for Alena's sake and for the sake of the foxes and martens and all the rest, and for my own sake too: with each step I took I could feel my consciousness expanding like a balloon, the breath of saintliness seeping steadily into me. Up to this point I'd worn suede and leather like anybody else, ankle boots and Air Jordans, a bombardier jacket I'd had since high school. If I'd drawn the line with fur, it was only because I'd never had any use for it. If I lived in the Yukon – and sometimes, drowsing through a meeting at work, I found myself fantasizing about it – I would have worn fur, no compunction, no second thoughts.

But not anymore. Now I was a protestor, a placard waver, now I was fighting for the right of every last weasel and lynx to grow old and die gracefully, now I was Alena Jorgensen's lover and a force to be reckoned with. Of course, my feet hurt and I was running

1 **immaculate:** tadellos, blitzblank.
4 **conspicuous:** auffällig, auffallend, unübersehbar.
6 **marten:** Marder.
8 **saintliness:** Heiligkeit.
11 **Air Jordans:** Basketballsportschuhe.
12 **to draw the line:** den Schlussstrich ziehen.
14 **Yukon:** nordkanadischer Bundesstaat.
to drowse: (vor sich hin)dösen.
16 **no compunction:** ohne Schuldgefühle.
19 **lynx:** Luchs.
20f. **to be reckoned with:** mit der, dem man rechnen muss.

sweat and praying that no one from work would drive by and see me there on the sidewalk with my crazy cohorts and denunciatory sign.

We marched for hours, back and forth, till I thought we'd wear a groove in the pavement. We chanted and jeered and nobody so much as looked at us twice. We could have been Hare Krishnas, bums, antiabortionists or lepers, what did it matter? To the rest of the world, to the uninitiated masses to whose sorry number I'd belonged just twenty-four hours earlier, we were invisible. I was hungry, tired, discouraged. Alena was ignoring me. Even the woman in red-face was slowing down, her chant a hoarse whisper that was sucked up and obliterated in the roar of traffic. And then, as the afternoon faded toward rush hour, a wizened silvery old woman who might have been an aging star or a star's mother or

3 **cohort:** Kohorte, Trupp.
denunciatory sign: Zeichen der Denunziation, Anprangerung.
5 **to wear a groove in the pavement:** eine Furche in den Bürgersteig graben.
6 **to jeer:** höhnen, buhen.
7 **Hare Krishnas** (pl.): Anhänger der Religionsgemeinschaft, die den Lehren von Bhaktivedanta Swami Prabhupada folgt.
bum (coll.): Penner, Rumtreiber.
8 **antiabortionist:** Abtreibungsgegner(in).
leper: Leprakranke(r)
9 **uninitiated:** nicht eingeweiht, ahnungslos.
10 **sorry number:** bedauernswerte Ansammlung.
13 **hoarse:** heiser.
14 **to suck s.th. up:** etwas aufsaugen, verschlucken.
to obliterate s.th.: etwas auslöschen, tilgen.
16 **wizened:** verhutzelt.

even the first dimly remembered wife of a studio exec got out of a long white car at the curb and strode fearlessly toward us. Despite the heat – it must have been eighty degrees at this point – she was wearing an ankle-length silver fox coat, a bristling shouldery wafting mass of peltry that must have decimated every burrow on the tundra. It was the moment we'd been waiting for.

A cry went up, shrill and ululating, and we converged on the lone old woman like a Cheyenne war party scouring the plains. The man beside me went down on all fours and howled like a dog, Alena slashed the air with her limp mink and the blood sang in my ears. "Murderer!" I screamed, getting into it. "Torturer! Nazi!" The strings in my neck were tight. I didn't know what I was saying. The crowd gibbered. The placards danced. I was so close to the old woman I could smell her – her perfume, a whiff of mothballs

1 **studio exec:** Studioboss (*exec:* Kurzform von *executioner*).
2 **curb:** Bordsteinkante.
5 **bristling:** borstig.
6 **to waft:** wehen.
peltry: Pelzwaren, Felle.
7 **burrow:** Bau, Höhle.
9 **ululating:** klagend.
9f. **to converge on s.o.:** auf jdn. zulaufen.
10 **lone:** einsam.
Cheyenne: nordamerikanischer Indianerstamm.
11 **to scour:** durchkämmen, -streifen.
13 **to slash the air with s.th.:** wild mit etwas in der Luft herumfuchteln.
15 **string:** Sehne.
16 **to gibber:** schnattern.
18 **mothball:** Mottenkugel.

from the coat – and it intoxicated me, maddened me, and I stepped in front of her and blocked her path with all the seething militant bulk of my one hundred eighty-five pounds of sinew and muscle.

I never saw the chauffeur. Alena told me afterward that he was a former kickboxing champion who'd been banned from the sport for excessive brutality. The first blow seemed to drop down from above, a shell lobbed from deep within enemy territory; the others came at me like a windmill churning in a storm. Someone screamed. I remember focusing on the flawless rigid pleats of the chauffeur's trousers, and then things got a bit hazy.

I woke to the dull thump of the surf slamming at the shore and the touch of Alena's lips on my own. I felt as if I'd been broken on the wheel, dismantled and put back together again. "Lie still," she said, and her tongue moved against my swollen cheek. Stricken, I could only drag my head across the pillow and gaze

1 **to intoxicate:** berauschen.
3 **seething:** wütend, wutentbrannt.
bulk: Masse.
4 **sinew:** Sehne.
9 **to lob s.th.:** etwas im hohen Bogen werfen.
10 **to churn:** sich wild drehen.
12 **pleat:** Falte.
13 **hazy:** verschwommen.
14 **thump:** (dumpfer) Schlag.
16 **to break s.o. on the wheel:** jdn. rädern, jdm. die Gliedmaßen zerschmettern.
dismantled: auseinander genommen.
18 **stricken:** verwundet, leidend.
19 **to gaze:** starren.

into the depths of her parti-colored eyes. "You're one of us now," she whispered.

Next morning I didn't even bother to call in sick.

By the end of the week I'd recovered enough to crave meat, for which I felt deeply ashamed, and to wear out a pair of vinyl huaraches on the picket line. Together, and with various coalitions of antivivisectionists, militant Vegans and cat lovers, Alena and I tramped a hundred miles of sidewalk, spray-painted inflammatory slogans across the windows of supermarkets and burger stands, denounced tanners, furriers, poulterers and sausage makers, and somehow found time to break up a cockfight in Pacoima. It was exhilarating, heady, dangerous. If I'd been disconnected in the past, I was plugged in now. I felt righteous – for the first time in my life I had a cause – and I had Alena, Alena above all. She fascinated me, fixated me, made me feel like a tomcat leaping in and

1 **parti-colored:** bunt.
4 **to crave s.th.:** sich nach etwas sehnen.
6 **huaraches** (Mex. Span.): Riemchensandalen.
picket line: Streikpostenkette.
7f. **antivivisectionist:** Gegner(in) der Vivisektion (Operation an lebenden Tieren).
10 **inflammatory:** aufrührerisch, aufwieglerisch.
11 **to denounce:** denunzieren, anprangern.
12 **poulterer:** Geflügelhändler.
13 **Pacoima:** Ortschaft im San Fernando Valley nordöstlich von Los Angeles.
14 **exhilarating:** aufregend.
heady: berauschend.
18 **tomcat:** Kater.

out of second-story windows, oblivious to the free-fall and the picket fence below. There was her beauty, of course, a triumph of evolution and the happy interchange of genes going all the way back to the cavemen, but it was more than that – it was her commitment to animals, to the righting of wrongs, to morality that made her irresistible. Was it love? The term is something I've always had difficulty with, but I suppose it was. Sure it was. Love, pure and simple. I had it, it had me.

"You know what?" Alena said one night as she stood over the miniature stove, searing tofu in oil and garlic. We'd spent the afternoon demonstrating out front of a tortilla factory that used rendered animal fat as a congealing agent, after which we'd been chased three blocks by an overweight assistant manager at Von's who objected to Alena's spray-painting MEAT IS DEATH over the specials in the front window. I was giddy with the adolescent joy of it. I sank into the couch with a beer and watched Alf limp across the floor to fling himself down and lick at a

1 *(to be)* **oblivious to s.th.:** sich etwas nicht bewusst machen.
2 **picket fence:** Palisadenzaun.
5f. **commitment:** Engagement.
7 **irresistible:** unwiderstehlich.
12 **to sear:** rasch anbraten
13 **garlic:** Knoblauch.
14 **rendered:** ausgelassen (Fett).
15 **congealing agent:** Bindemittel.
19 **giddy:** schwindlig.
20 **to limp:** hinken, humpeln.
21 **to fling o.s. down:** sich auf den Boden fallen lassen.

suspicious spot on the floor. The surf boomed like thunder.

"What?" I said.

"Thanksgiving's coming."

I let it ride a moment, wondering if I should invite Alena to my mother's for the big basted bird stuffed with canned oysters and buttered bread crumbs, and then realized it probably wouldn't be such a great idea. I said nothing.

She glanced over her shoulder. "The animals don't have a whole lot to be thankful for, that's for sure. It's just an excuse for the meat industry to butcher a couple million turkeys, is all it is." She paused; hot safflower oil popped in the pan. "I think it's time for a little road trip," she said. "Can we take your car?"

"Sure, but where are we going?"

She gave me her Gioconda smile. "To liberate some turkeys."

In the morning I called my boss to tell him I had pancreatic cancer and wouldn't be in for a while, then we threw some things in the car, helped Alf scrabble into the back seat, and headed up Route 5 for the San Joa-

1 **to boom:** dröhnen.
6 **to baste s.th.:** etwas mit Fett beträufeln.
7 **oyster:** Auster.
14 **safflower:** Saflor, Färberdistel.
17 **Gioconda smile:** Mona-Lisa-Lächeln.
19 f. **pancreatic cancer:** Bauchspeicheldrüsenkrebs.
21 **to scrabble:** klettern.
22 f. **San Joaquin Valley:** fruchtbares Tal in Kalifornien, auch »Golden Valley« genannt.

quin Valley. We drove for three hours through a fog so dense the windows might as well have been packed with cotton. Alena was secretive, but I could see she was excited. I knew only that we were on our way to rendezvous with a certain "Rolfe," a longtime friend of hers and a big name in the world of ecotage and animal rights, after which we would commit some desperate and illegal act, for which the turkeys would be eternally grateful.

There was a truck stalled in front of the sign for our exit at Calpurnia Springs, and I had to brake hard and jerk the wheel around twice to keep the tires on the pavement. Alena came up out of her seat and Alf slammed into the armrest like a sack of meal, but we made it. A few minutes later we were gliding through the ghostly vacancy of the town itself, lights drifting past in a nimbus of fog, glowing pink, yellow and white, and then there was only the blacktop road and the pale void that engulfed it. We'd gone ten miles or so when Alena instructed me to slow down and began to study the right-hand shoulder with a keen, unwavering eye.

3 **secretive:** (fig.) verschlossen.
6 **ecotage:** Sabotageakte von Umweltschützern.
10 **stalled:** liegen geblieben (Auto).
14 **meal:** Schrotmehl.
16 **vacancy:** Leere.
17 **nimbus:** Heiligenschein.
18 **blacktop road:** geteerte Straße.
19 **void:** Leere.
to engulf: verschlingen.
21 **shoulder:** Rand-, Seitenstreifen (Straße).
21 f. **unwavering:** beharrlich.

The earth breathed in and out. I squinted hard into the soft drifting glow of the headlights. "There, there!" she cried and I swung the wheel to the right, and suddenly we were lurching along a pitted dirt road that rose up from the blacktop like a goat path worn into the side of a mountain. Five minutes later Alf sat up in the back seat and began to whine, and then a crude unpainted shack began to detach itself from the vagueness around us.

Rolfe met us on the porch. He was tall and leathery, in his fifties, I guessed, with a shock of hair and rutted features that brought Samuel Beckett to mind. He was wearing gumboots and jeans and a faded lumberjack shirt that looked as if it had been washed a hundred times. Alf took a quick pee against the side of the house, then fumbled up the steps to roll over and fawn at his feet.

"Rolfe!" Alena called, and there was too much animation in her voice, too much familiarity, for my taste. She took the steps in a bound and threw herself

1 **to squint:** blinzeln.
4 **pitted:** mit Schlaglöchern übersät.
4f. **dirt road:** unbefestigte Straße.
7 **to whine:** jaulen.
8 **shack:** Hütte.
10 **porch:** Veranda.
11 **shock of hair:** Haarschopf.
12 **rutted:** zerfurcht.
Beckett: Samuel B. (1906–89), irischer Dramatiker.
14 **lumberjack:** Holzfäller.
17 **to fawn:** herumscharwenzeln.
18f. **animation:** Lebhaftigkeit.
20 **in a bound:** mit einem Satz.

in his arms. I watched them kiss, and it wasn't a fatherly-daughterly sort of kiss, not at all. It was a kiss with some meaning behind it, and I didn't like it. Rolfe, I thought: What kind of name is that?

"Rolfe," Alena gasped, still a little breathless from bouncing up the steps like a cheerleader, "I'd like you to meet Jim."

This was my signal. I ascended the porch steps and held out my hand. Rolfe gave me a look out of the hooded depths of his eyes and then took my hand in a hard callused grip, the grip of the wood splitter, the fence mender, the liberator of hothouse turkeys and laboratory mice. "A pleasure," he said, and his voice rasped like sandpaper.

There was a fire going inside, and Alena and I sat before it and warmed our hands while Alf whined and sniffed and Rolfe served Red Zinger tea in Japanese cups the size of thimbles. Alena hadn't stopped chattering since we stepped through the door, and Rolfe came right back at her in his woodsy rasp, the two of them exchanging names and news and gossip as if they were talking in code. I studied the reproduc-

5 **to gasp:** keuchen.
6 **to bounce:** springen.
8 **to ascend:** hinaufsteigen.
10 **hooded:** mit schweren Lidern, halb geschlossen.
11 **callused:** schwielig.
14 **to rasp:** schmirgeln, rau klingen.
17 **Red Zinger tea:** Kräutertee aus Hibiskus, Hagebutte, Zitronengras und Süßholz.
18 **thimble:** Fingerhut.
20 **woodsy:** wäldlerisch.

tions of teal and widgeon that hung from the peeling walls, noted the case of Heinz vegetarian beans in the corner and the half-gallon of Jack Daniel's on the mantel. Finally, after the third cup of tea, Alena settled back in her chair – a huge old Salvation Army sort of thing with a soiled antimacassar – and said, "So what's the plan?"

Rolfe gave me another look, a quick predatory darting of the eyes, as if he weren't sure I could be trusted, and then turned back to Alena. "Hedda Gabler's Range-Fed Turkey Ranch," he said. "And no, I don't find the name cute, not at all." He looked at me now, a long steady assay. "They grind up the heads for cat food, and the neck, the organs and the rest, that they wrap up in paper and stuff back in the body cavity like it was a war atrocity or something. Whatever did a turkey go and do to us to deserve a fate like that?"

The question was rhetorical, even if it seemed to have been aimed at me, and I made no response

1 **teal:** Krickente.
widgeon: Pfeifente.
to peel: abblättern (Tapete, Farbe).
3 **Jack Daniel's:** Whiskymarke.
4 **mantel:** Kaminsims.
5 **Salvation Army:** Heilsarmee.
6 **soiled:** schmutzig.
antimacassar: Sesselschoner.
8f. **predatory darting:** raubtierartiges Blitzen.
13 **assay:** prüfender Blick.
16 **cavity:** Höhlung.
war atrocity: Kriegsgräueltat.

other than to compose my face in a look that wedded grief, outrage and resolve. I was thinking of all the turkeys I'd sent to their doom, of the plucked wishbones, the pope's noses and the crisp browned skin I used to relish as a kid. It brought a lump to my throat, and something more: I realized I was hungry.

"Ben Franklin wanted to make them our national symbol," Alena chimed in, "did you know that? But the meat eaters won out."

"Fifty thousand birds," Rolfe said, glancing at Alena and bringing his incendiary gaze back to rest on me. "I have information they're going to start slaughtering them tomorrow, for the fresh-not-frozen market."

"Yuppie poultry." Alena's voice was drenched in disgust.

For a moment, no one spoke. I became aware of the crackling of the fire. The fog pressed at the windows. It was getting dark.

1 **to compose one's face:** sich wieder in die Gewalt bekommen.
to wed: kombinieren.
2 **outrage:** Empörung.
3 **doom:** Schicksal; Verderben.
3f. **wishbone:** Gabelbein.
4 **pope's nose:** Bürzel.
crisp: knusprig.
7 **Franklin:** Benjamin F. (1706–90), Unterzeichner der Unabhängigkeitserklärung und der Verfassung der USA.
8 **to chime in** (coll.): sich einschalten.
11 **incendiary gaze:** brennender Blick.
13 **to slaughter:** schlachten.
15f. **drenched in disgust** (fig.): voller Ekel.
18 **crackling:** Knistern.

"You can see the place from the highway," Rolfe said finally, "but the only access is through Calpurnia Springs. It's about twenty miles – twenty-two point three, to be exact."

Alena's eyes were bright. She was gazing on Rolfe as if he'd just dropped down from heaven. I felt something heave in my stomach.

"We strike tonight."

Rolfe insisted that we take my car – "Everybody around here knows my pickup, and I can't take any chances on a little operation like this" – but we did mask the plates, front and back, with an inch-thick smear of mud. We blackened our faces like commandos and collected our tools from the shed out back – tin snips, a crowbar and two five-gallon cans of gasoline. "Gasoline?" I said, trying the heft of the can. Rolfe gave me a craggy look. "To create a diversion," he said. Alf, for obvious reasons, stayed behind in the shack.

If the fog had been thick in daylight, it was impermeable now, the sky collapsed upon the earth. It took

7 **to heave:** sich heben und senken, aufwallen.
12 **plates** (coll.): Nummernschilder.
13 **smear:** Schmierfleck.
13 f. **commando:** Mitglied eines Kommandotrupps.
15 **tin snips** (pl.): Drahtschere.
crowbar: Brecheisen.
16 **heft:** Gewicht.
17 **craggy:** schroff.
diversion: Ablenkung(smanöver).
20 f. **impermeable:** undurchlässig, undurchdringlich.

hold of the headlights and threw them back at me till my eyes began to water from the effort of keeping the car on the road. But for the ruts and bumps we might have been floating in space. Alena sat up front between Rolfe and me, curiously silent. Rolfe didn't have much to say either, save for the occasional grunted command: "Hang a right here"; "Hard left"; "Easy, easy." I thought about meat and jail and the heroic proportions to which I was about to swell in Alena's eyes and what I intended to do to her when we finally got to bed. It was 2:00 A. M. by the dashboard clock.

"Okay," Rolfe said, and his voice came at me so suddenly it startled me, "pull over here – and kill the lights."

We stepped out into the hush of night and eased the doors shut behind us. I couldn't see a thing, but I could hear the not-so-distant hiss of traffic on the highway, and another sound, too, muffled and indistinct, the gentle unconscious suspiration of thousands upon thousands of my fellow creatures. And I could smell them, a seething rancid odor of feces and

3 **rut:** Schlagloch.
11 f. **dashboard:** Armaturenbrett.
14 f. **to kill the lights:** die Scheinwerfer ausschalten.
16 **hush:** Stille.
18 **hiss:** Zischen, Rauschen.
19 **muffled:** gedämpft.
19 f. **indistinct:** undeutlich.
20 **suspiration:** Seufzen.
22 **seething** (fig.): brodelnd.
rancid: ranzig.
feces (pl.): Kot.

feathers and naked scaly feet that crawled down my throat and burned my nostrils. "Whew," I said in a whisper, "I can smell them."

Rolfe and Alena were vague presences at my side. Rolfe flipped open the trunk and in the next moment I felt the heft of a crowbar and a pair of tin snips in my hand. "Listen, you, Jim," Rolfe whispered, taking me by the wrist in his iron grip and leading me half-a-dozen steps forward. "Feel this?"

I felt a grid of wire, which he promptly cut: *snip, snip, snip*.

"This is their enclosure – they're out there in the day, scratching around in the dirt. You get lost, you follow this wire. Now, you're going to take a section out of this side, Alena's got the west side and I've got the south. Once that's done I signal with the flashlight and we bust open the doors to the turkey houses – they're these big low white buildings, you'll see them when you get close – and flush the birds out. Don't worry about me or Alena. Just worry about getting as many birds out as you can."

I was worried. Worried about everything, from some half-crazed farmer with a shotgun or AK 47 or whatever they carried these days, to losing Alena in the fog, to the turkeys themselves: How big were they? Were they violent? They had claws and beaks,

1 **scaly:** schuppig.
10 **grid:** Gitter.
12 **enclosure:** Gehege.
19 **to flush:** (auf-, hinaus)scheuchen.
23 **AK 47:** Sturmgewehr.

didn't they? And how were they going to feel about me bursting into their bedroom in the middle of the night?

"And when the gas cans go up, you hightail it back to the car, got it?"

I could hear the turkeys tossing in their sleep. A truck shifted gears out on the highway. "I think so," I whispered.

"And one more thing – be sure to leave the keys in the ignition."

This gave me pause. "But –"

"The getaway." Alena was so close I could feel her breath on my ear. "I mean, we don't want to be fumbling around for the keys when all hell is breaking loose out there, do we?"

I eased open the door and reinserted the keys in the ignition, even though the automatic buzzer warned me against it. "Okay," I murmured, but they were already gone, soaked up in the shadows and the mist. At this point my heart was hammering so loudly I could barely hear the rustling of the turkeys – this is crazy, I told myself, it's hurtful and wrong, not to mention illegal. Spray-painting slogans was one thing, but this was something else altogether. I thought of

4 **to hightail it** (coll.): abhauen.
6 **to toss:** sich unruhig hin und her bewegen.
10 **ignition:** Zündschloss.
12 **getaway:** Flucht.
13 f. **to fumble around for s.th.:** nach etwas tasten, herumsuchen.
17 **buzzer:** Summer, Summton.
19 **soaked up:** (fig.) verschluckt.
21 **rustling:** Rascheln.

the turkey farmer asleep in his bed, an entrepreneur working to make America strong, a man with a wife and kids and a mortgage … but then I thought of all those innocent turkeys consigned to death, and finally I thought of Alena, long-legged and loving, and the way she came to me out of the darkness of the bathroom and the boom of the surf. I took the tin snips to the wire.

I must have been at it half an hour, forty-five minutes, gradually working my way toward the big white sheds that had begun to emerge from the gloom up ahead, when I saw Rolfe's flashlight blinking off to my left. This was my signal to head to the nearest shed, snap off the padlock with my crowbar, fling open the doors and herd a bunch of cranky suspicious gobblers out into the night. It was now or never. I looked twice round me and then broke for the near shed in an awkward crouching gait. The turkeys must have sensed that something was up – from behind the long white windowless wall there arose a watchful gabbling, a soughing of feathers that fanned up like a

1 **entrepreneur:** Unternehmer.
3 **mortgage:** Hypothek.
4 **consigned to death:** für den Tod bestimmt, todgeweiht.
11 **gloom:** Dunkel.
14 **padlock:** Vorhängeschloss.
14f. **to fling open:** aufreißen.
15 **cranky:** verrückt.
16 **gobbler** (coll.): Truthahn.
18 **crouching gait:** leicht gebückter Gang.
21 **gabbling:** Kollern.
soughing: Rauschen, Rascheln.

breeze in the treetops. *Hold on, you toms and hens,* I thought, *freedom is at hand.* A jerk of the wrist, and the padlock fell to the ground. Blood pounding in my ears, I took hold of the sliding door and jerked it open with a great dull booming reverberation – and suddenly, there they were, turkeys, thousands upon thousands of them, cloaked in white feathers under a string of dim yellow bulbs. The light glinted in their reptilian eyes. Somewhere a dog began to bark.

I steeled myself and sprang through the door with a shout, whirling the crowbar over my head. "All right!" I boomed, and the echo gave it back to me a hundred times over, "this is it! Turkeys, on your feet!" Nothing. No response. But for the whisper of rustling feathers and the alertly cocked heads, they might have been sculptures, throw pillows, they might as well have been dead and butchered and served up with yams and onions and all the trimmings. The barking of the dog went up a notch. I thought I heard voices.

The turkeys crouched on the concrete floor, wave upon wave of them, stupid and immovable; they

2 **jerk:** Ruck, ruckartige Bewegung.
3 **to pound:** hämmern.
4 **sliding door:** Schiebetür.
7 **cloaked:** gehüllt.
10 **to steel o.s.:** sich wappnen.
11 **to whirl:** wirbeln.
15 **alertly** (adv.): wachsam.
17 **yam:** Süßkartoffel.
18 **and all the trimmings:** mit allen Beilagen.
19 **to go up a notch:** eine Spur lauter werden.
20 **to crouch:** hocken, kauern.

perched in the rafters, on shelves and platforms, huddled in wooden stalls. Desperate, I rushed into the front rank of them, swinging my crowbar, stamping my feet and howling like the wishbone plucker I once was. That did it. There was a shriek from the nearest bird and the others took it up till an unholy racket filled the place, and now they were moving, tumbling down from their perches, flapping their wings in a storm of dried excrement and pecked-over grain, pouring across the concrete floor till it vanished beneath them. Encouraged, I screamed again – "Yeeee-ha-ha-ha-ha!" – and beat at the aluminum walls with the crowbar as the turkeys shot through the doorway and out into the night.

It was then that the black mouth of the doorway erupted with light and the *ka-boom!* of the gas cans sent a tremor through the earth. *Run!* a voice screamed in my head, and the adrenaline kicked in and all of a sudden I was scrambling for the door in a hurricane of turkeys. They were everywhere, flapping their wings, gobbling and screeching, loosing their bowels in panic. Something hit the back of my legs and all at once I was down amongst them, on the floor, in the dirt and feathers and wet turkey shit. I was a roadbed, a turkey expressway. Their claws dug at my

1 **rafter:** Dachsparren.
5 **shriek:** Kreischen.
8 **perch:** Sitzstange.
to flap one's wings: mit den Flügeln flattern.
16 **to erupt:** aus-, aufbrechen.
21 **to screech:** kreischen.

back, my shoulders, the crown of my head. Panicked now, choking on feathers and dust and worse, I fought to my feet as the big screeching birds launched themselves round me, and staggered out into the barnyard. "There! Who's that there?" a voice roared, and I was off and running.

What can I say? I vaulted turkeys, kicked them aside like so many footballs, slashed and tore at them as they sailed through the air. I ran till my lungs felt as if they were burning right through my chest, disoriented, bewildered, terrified of the shotgun blast I was sure would cut me down at any moment. Behind me the fire raged and lit the fog till it glowed blood-red and hellish. But where was the fence? And where the car?

I got control of my feet then and stood stock-still in a flurry of turkeys, squinting into the wall of fog. Was that it? Was that the car over there? At that moment I heard an engine start up somewhere behind me – a familiar engine with a familiar coughing gurgle in the throat of the carburetor – and then the lights blinked on briefly three hundred yards away. I heard the engine race and listened, helpless, as the car roared off in the opposite direction. I stood there a moment

2 **to choke on s.th.:** fast an etwas ersticken.
3 f. **to launch o.s.:** sich stürzen.
4 **barnyard:** Hof.
7 **to vault:** überspringen.
8 **to slash at s.th.:** auf etwas losgehen.
11 **bewildered:** verwirrt.
17 **flurry:** Gestöber, Gewimmel.
21 **carburetor:** Vergaser.

longer, forlorn and forsaken, and then I ran blindly off into the night, putting the fire and the shouts and the barking and the incessant mindless squawking of the turkeys as far behind me as I could.

When dawn finally broke, it was only just perceptibly, so thick was the fog. I'd made my way to a blacktop road – which road and where it led I didn't know – and sat crouched and shivering in a clump of weed just off the shoulder. Alena wouldn't desert me, I was sure of that – she loved me, as I loved her; needed me, as I needed her – and I was sure she'd be cruising along the back roads looking for me. My pride was wounded, of course, and if I never laid eyes on Rolfe again I felt I wouldn't be missing much, but at least I hadn't been drilled full of shot, savaged by farm dogs or pecked to death by irate turkeys. I was sore all over, my shin throbbed where I'd slammed into something substantial while vaulting through the night, there were feathers in my hair and my face and arms were a mosaic of cuts and scratches and long trailing fissures of dirt. I'd been sitting there for what seemed

1 **forlorn and forsaken:** total verlassen.
3 **incessant:** unaufhörlich.
squawking: Gackern.
5 **perceptibly** (adv.): wahrnehmbar, sichtbar.
8 **to shiver:** zittern, beben.
clump: Büschel, Haufen.
15 **drilled full of shot:** mit Schrotkugeln voll gepumpt.
16 **irate:** wütend.
17 **shin:** Schienbein.
to throb: hämmern, pochen.
20f. **long trailing fissures of dirt:** lang gezogene Dreckspuren.

like hours, cursing Rolfe, developing suspicions about Alena and unflattering theories about environmentalists in general, when finally I heard the familiar slurp and roar of my Chevy Citation cutting through the mist ahead of me.

Rolfe was driving, his face impassive. I flung myself into the road like a tattered beggar, waving my arms over my head and giving vent to my joy, and he very nearly ran me down. Alena was out of the car before it stopped, wrapping me up in her arms, and then she was bundling me into the rear seat with Alf and we were on our way back to the hideaway. "What happened?" she cried, as if she couldn't have guessed. "Where were you? We waited as long as we could."

I was feeling sulky, betrayed, feeling as if I was owed a whole lot more than a perfunctory hug and a string of insipid questions. Still, as I told my tale I began to warm to it – they'd got away in the car with the heater going, and I'd stayed behind to fight the turkeys, the farmers and the elements, too, and if that wasn't heroic, I'd like to know what was. I looked into Alena's admiring eyes and pictured Rolfe's shack, a

2 **unflattering:** wenig schmeichelhaft.
2 f. **environmentalist:** Umweltschützer(in).
3 **slurp:** Schlürfen.
4 **Chevy Citation:** Auto der Marke Chevrolet, gebaut in den 1980er-Jahren.
7 **tattered:** zerlumpt.
8 **to give vent to one's joy:** seiner Freude freien Lauf lassen.
15 **sulky:** beleidigt, schmollend.
betrayed: verraten.
16 **perfunctory:** flüchtig.
17 **insipid:** langweilig, geistlos.

nip or two from the bottle of Jack Daniel's, maybe a peanut-butter-and-tofu sandwich and then the bed, with Alena in it. Rolfe said nothing.

Back at Rolfe's, I took a shower and scrubbed the turkey droppings from my pores, then helped myself to the bourbon. It was ten in the morning and the house was dark – if the world had ever been without fog, there was no sign of it here. When Rolfe stepped out on the porch to fetch an armload of firewood, I pulled Alena down into my lap. "Hey," she murmured, "I thought you were an invalid."

She was wearing a pair of too-tight jeans and an oversize sweater with nothing underneath it. I slipped my hand inside the sweater and found something to hold on to. "Invalid?" I said, nuzzling at her sleeve. "Hell, I'm a turkey liberator, an ecoguerrilla, a friend of the animals and the environment, too."

She laughed, but she pushed herself up and crossed the room to stare out the occluded window. "Listen, Jim," she said, "what we did last night was great, really great, but it's just the beginning." Alf looked up at her expectantly. I heard Rolfe fumbling around on the porch, the thump of wood on wood. She turned round to face me now. "What I mean is, Rolfe wants me to go up to Wyoming for a little bit, just outside of Yellowstone –"

15 **to nuzzle at s.th.:** an etwas nesteln, (behutsam) gegen etwas drücken.

19 **occluded:** geschlossen.

26 **Yellowstone:** bekannter Nationalpark in Kalifornien mit einer Fläche von 8983 km², gegründet 1872; den Namen hat er wegen der gelben Felsen am Grand Canyon bekommen.

Me? Rolfe wants me? There was no invitation in that, no plurality, no acknowledgment of all we'd done and meant to each other. "For what?" I said. "What do you mean?"

"There's this grizzly – a pair of them, actually – and they've been raiding places outside the park. One of them made off with the mayor's Doberman the other night and the people are up in arms. We – I mean Rolfe and me and some other people from the old Bolt Weevils in Minnesota? – we're going to go up there and make sure the Park Service – or the local yahoos – don't eliminate them. The bears, I mean."

My tone was corrosive. "You and Rolfe?"

"There's nothing between us, if that's what you're thinking. This has to do with animals, that's all."

"Like us?"

She shook her head slowly. "Not like us, no. We're the plague on this planet, don't you know that?"

Suddenly I was angry. Seething. Here I'd crouched in the bushes all night, covered in turkey crap, and now I was part of a plague. I was on my feet. "No, I don't know that."

She gave me a look that let me know it didn't matter, that she was already gone, that her agenda, at least for the moment, didn't include me and there was

8 **to be up in arms:** empört sein.
10 **Bolt Weevils:** Gruppe von Ökoaktivisten (*weevil:* Rüsselkäfer).
11 f. **local yahoos** (pl.): ignorante Einheimische.
13 **corrosive:** ätzend.
18 **plague:** Pest, Seuche.
20 **crap** (vulg.): Scheiße.
24 **agenda:** Tagesordnung, Plan; (heimliche) Absichten.

no use arguing about it. "Look," she said, her voice dropping as Rolfe slammed back through the door with a load of wood, "I'll see you in L. A. in a month or so, okay?" She gave me an apologetic smile. "Water the plants for me?"

An hour later I was on the road again. I'd helped Rolfe stack the wood beside the fireplace, allowed Alena to brush my lips with a goodbye kiss, and then stood there on the porch while Rolfe locked up, lifted Alf into the bed of his pickup and rumbled down the rutted dirt road with Alena at his side. I watched till their brake lights dissolved in the drifting gray mist, then fired up the Citation and lurched down the road behind them. *A month or so:* I felt hollow inside. I pictured her with Rolfe, eating yogurt and wheat germ, stopping at motels, wrestling grizzlies and spiking trees. The hollowness opened up, cored me out till I felt as if I'd been plucked and gutted and served up on a platter myself.

I found my way back through Calpurnia Springs without incident – there were no roadblocks, no flashing lights and grim-looking troopers searching trunks

4 **apologetic:** entschuldigend; zaghaft.
7 **to stack:** (auf)stapeln.
12 **to dissolve:** sich auflösen, verschwinden.
13 **to fire up** (coll.): starten.
15 f. **wheat germ:** Weizenkeime.
17 **to core s.o. out:** jdn. entkernen, aushöhlen.
18 **plucked and gutted:** gerupft und ausgenommen.
22 **trooper:** Polizist.

and back seats for a tallish thirty-year-old ecoterrorist with turkey tracks down his back – but after I turned onto the highway for Los Angeles, I had a shock. Ten miles up the road my nightmare materialized out of the gloom: red lights everywhere, signal flares and police cars lined up on the shoulder. I was on the very edge of panicking, a beat away from cutting across the meridian and giving them a run for it, when I saw the truck jackknifed up ahead. I slowed to forty, thirty, and then hit the brakes again. In a moment I was stalled in a line of cars and there was something all over the road, ghostly and white in the fog. At first I thought it must have been flung from the truck, rolls of toilet paper or crates of soap powder ruptured on the pavement. It was neither. As I inched closer, the tires creeping now, the pulse of the lights in my face, I saw that the road was coated in feathers, turkey feathers. A storm of them. A blizzard. And more: there was flesh there too, slick and greasy, a red pulp ground into the surface of the road, thrown up like slush from the tires of the car ahead of me, ground

1 **tallish:** ziemlich groß (Person).
5 **signal flare:** Leuchtsignal.
7 f. **to cut across the meridian:** auf die Gegenfahrbahn wechseln (*meridian:* Mittelstreifen).
9 **jackknifed:** quer über die Fahrbahn gestellt.
14 **crate:** Kiste.
ruptured: aufgerissen, geplatzt, auseinander gebrochen.
19 **slick:** rutschig.
greasy: schmierig.
pulp: Brei.
21 **slush:** Matsch.

beneath the massive wheels of the truck. Turkeys. Turkeys everywhere.

The car crept forward. I flicked on the windshield wipers, hit the washer button, and for a moment a scrim of diluted blood obscured the windows and the hollowness opened up inside of me till I thought it would suck me inside out. Behind me, someone was leaning on his horn. A trooper loomed up out of the gloom, waving me on with the dead yellow eye of his flashlight. I thought of Alena and felt sick. All there was between us had come to this, expectations gone sour, a smear on the road. I wanted to get out and shoot myself, turn myself in, close my eyes and wake up in jail, in a hair shirt, in a straitjacket, anything. It went on. Time passed. Nothing moved. And then, miraculously, a vision began to emerge from behind the smeared glass and the gray belly of the fog, lights glowing golden in the waste. I saw the sign, Gas/Food/Lodging, and my hand was on the blinker.

It took me a moment, picturing the place, the generic tile, the false cheer of the lights, the odor of charred flesh hanging heavy on the air, Big Mac, three-piece dark meat, carne asada, cheeseburger.

5 **scrim:** Schleier, Schicht.
diluted: verdünnt.
to obscure: verdecken, verdunkeln.
14 **hair shirt:** härenes Hemd, Härenhemd; Büßerhemd.
straitjacket: Zwangsjacke.
20 f. **generic tile:** typischer Ziegel.
22 **charred:** verkohlt.
23 **carne asada:** mexikanisches Fleischgericht aus Rindsfiletwürfeln mit Tomaten, Chili und Koriander.

The engine coughed. The lights glowed. I didn't think of Alena then, didn't think of Rolfe or grizzlies or the doomed bleating flocks and herds, or of the blind bunnies and cancerous mice – I thought only of the cavern opening inside me and how to fill it. "Meat," and I spoke the word aloud, talking to calm myself as if I'd awakened from a bad dream, "it's only meat."

3 **to bleat:** blöken.
4 **cancerous:** krebskrank.
5 **cavern:** Höhle.

After the Plague

After the plague – it was some sort of Ebola mutation passed from hand to hand and nose to nose like the common cold – life was different. More relaxed and expansive, more natural. The rat race was over, the freeways were clear all the way to Sacramento, and the poor dwindling ravaged planet was suddenly big and mysterious again. It was a kind of miracle really, what the environmentalists had been hoping for all along, though of course even the most strident of them wouldn't have wished for his own personal extinction, but there it was. I don't mean to sound callous – my parents are long dead and I'm unmarried and siblingless, but I lost friends, colleagues and

1 **plague:** Seuche.
2 **Ebola mutation:** Mutation des Ebola-Virus (der das Ebola-Fieber überträgt, eine hoch infektiöse Erkrankung, die meist tödlich verläuft).
5 **expansive:** (fig.) offen.
rat race: ständiger Konkurrenzkampf.
6 **freeway:** Autobahn.
7 **to dwindle:** dahinschwinden, herunterkommen; zur Neige gehen (Bodenschätze).
ravaged: verwüstet, geplündert.
9 **environmentalist:** Umweltschützer(in).
10 **strident:** lautstark.
11 f. **extinction:** Auslöschung, Ausrottung.
12 f. **callous:** herzlos, gefühllos.
14 **siblingless:** ohne Geschwister.

neighbors, the same as any other survivor. What few of us there are, that is. We're guessing it's maybe one in ten thousand, here in the States anyway. I'm sure there are whole tribes that escaped it somewhere in the Amazon or the interior valleys of Indonesia, meteorologists in isolated weather stations, fire lookouts, goatherds and the like. But the president's gone, the vice president, the cabinet, Congress, the joint chiefs of staff, the chairmen of the boards and CEOs of the Fortune 500 companies, along with all their stockholders, employees and retainers. There's no TV. No electricity or running water. And there won't be any dining out anytime soon.

Actually, I'm lucky to be here to tell you about it – it was sheer serendipity, really. You see, I wasn't among my fellow human beings when it hit – no festering airline cabins or snaking supermarket lines for me, no concerts, sporting events or crowded restaurants – and the closest I came to intimate contact was a telephone call to my on-and-off girlfriend, Danielle, from a gas station in the Sierra foothills. I think I may

7 **goatherd:** Ziegenhirt.
9 **CEO:** Abk. für *chief executive officer:* Generaldirektor.
10 **Fortune 500 companies:** Liste der 500 größten amerikanischen Unternehmen, zusammengestellt von dem Wirtschaftsmagazin *Fortune.*
10f. **stockholder:** Aktionär.
11 **retainer:** Bevollmächtigte(r).
15 **sheer:** rein, glatt, absolut.
serendipity: mehr Glück als Verstand.
16f. **festering:** ansteckend, die Seuche verbreitend.
20 **on-and-off** (coll.): mit der ich mal zusammen bin, mal nicht.
21 **Sierra foothills** (pl.): Ausläufer der Sierra Nevada (600 km lange Gebirgskette in Kalifornien).

have made a kissing noise over the wire, my lips very possibly coming into contact with the molded plastic mouthpiece into which hordes of strangers had breathed before me, but this was a good two weeks before the first victim carried the great dripping bag of infection that was himself back from a camcorder safari to the Ngorongoro Crater or a conference on economic development in Malawi. Danielle, whose voice was a drug I was trying to kick, at least temporarily, promised to come join me for a weekend in the cabin after my six weeks of self-imposed isolation were over, but sadly, she never made it. Neither did anyone else.

I *was* isolated up there in the mountains – that was the whole point – and the first I heard of anything amiss was over the radio. It was a warm, full-bodied day in early fall, the sun caught like a child's ball in the crown of the Jeffrey pine outside the window, and I was washing up after lunch when a smooth melodious voice interrupted *Afternoon Classics* to say that people were bleeding from the eyeballs and vomiting up bile in the New York subways and collapsing en

2 **molded:** geformt.
7 **Ngorongoro Crater:** Riesenvulkankrater in Tanzania, 610 m tief, 260 km² breit (Naturschutzgebiet).
8 **Malawi:** Republik in Südostafrika.
9 **to kick a drug** (coll.): von einer Droge runterkommen.
16 **amiss:** nicht in Ordnung.
full-bodied: (fig.) gesättigt, erfüllt.
18 **Jeffrey pine:** Kiefernart.
22 **bile:** Galle.

masse in the streets of the capital. The authorities were fully prepared to deal with what they were calling a minor outbreak of swine flu, the voice said, and people were cautioned not to panic, but all at once the announcer seemed to chuckle deep in his throat, and then, right in the middle of the next phrase, he sneezed – a controlled explosion hurtling out over the airwaves to detonate ominously in ten million trembling speakers – and the radio fell silent. Somebody put on a CD of Richard Strauss' *Death and Transfiguration*, and it played over and over through the rest of the afternoon.

I didn't have access to a telephone – not unless I hiked two and a half miles out to the road where I'd parked my car and then drove another six to Fish Fry Flats, pop. 28, and used the public phone at the bar/restaurant/gift shop/one-stop grocery/gas station there – so I ran the dial up and down the radio to see if I could get some news. Reception is pretty spotty up in the mountains – you never knew whether you'd get Bakersfield, Fresno, San Luis Obispo or even Tijuana – and I couldn't pull in anything but white noise

3 **swine flu:** Schweinepest.
5 **to chuckle:** leise in sich hineinlachen.
7 f. **to hurtle out:** losbrausen.
8 **to detonate:** detonieren, zünden.
ominously (adv.): unheilvoll, bedrohlich.
10 f. **"Death and Transfiguration":** *Tod und Verklärung*, Tondichtung (op. 24) des deutschen Komponisten Richard Strauss (1864–1949).
16 **pop.:** Abk. für *population:* Einwohnerzahl.
18 **dial:** Skala (Radio).
19 **pretty spotty:** nur vereinzelt möglich.
22 **white noise:** (weißes) Rauschen.

on that particular afternoon, except for the aforementioned tone poem, that is. I was powerless. What would happen would happen, and I'd find out all the sordid details a week later, just as I found out about all the other crises, scandals, scoops, coups, typhoons, wars and cease-fires that held the world spellbound while I communed with the ground squirrels and woodpeckers. It was funny. The big events didn't seem to mean much up here in the mountains, where life was so much more elemental and immediate and the telling concerns of the day revolved around priming the water pump and lighting the balky old gas stove without blowing the place up. I picked up a worn copy of John Cheever's stories somebody had left in the cabin during one of its previous incarnations and forgot all about the news out of New York and Washington.

1 f. **aforementioned:** oben genannt.
4 **sordid:** eklig.
5 **scoop:** Knüller.
typhoon: Taifun, Wirbelsturm.
6 **cease-fire:** Waffenruhe.
spellbound: gebannt, wie verzaubert.
7 **to commune:** Zwiesprache halten.
ground squirrel: Erdhörnchen, Ziesel (Nagetier aus der Familie der Hörnchen).
8 **woodpecker:** Specht.
11 **telling concerns:** Hauptsorgen.
to revolve: sich drehen, kreisen.
11 f. **to prime:** (Pumpe) füllen.
12 **balky:** schwierig, bockig.
14 **Cheever:** John Ch. (1912–82), amerikanischer Schriftsteller, der hauptsächlich Kurzgeschichten verfasste.

Later, when it finally came to me that I couldn't live through another measure of Strauss without risk of permanent impairment, I flicked off the radio, put on a light jacket and went out to glory in the way the season had touched the aspens along the path out to the road. The sun was leaning way over to the west now, the shrubs and ground litter gathering up the night, the tall trees trailing deep blue shadows. There was the faintest breath of a chill in the air, a premonition of winter, and I thought of the simple pleasures of building a fire, preparing a homely meal and sitting through the evening with a book in one hand and a scotch and Drambuie in the other. It wasn't until nine or ten at night that I remembered the bleeding eyeballs and the fateful sneeze, and though I was half-convinced it was a hoax or maybe one of those fugitive terrorist attacks with a colorless, odorless gas – sarin or the like – I turned on the radio, eager for news.

1 **it came to me:** ich habe es kapiert.
3 **impairment:** Schaden, Beeinträchtigung.
5 **aspen:** Espe.
7 **shrub:** Busch, Strauch.
8 **to trail:** hinter sich herziehen.
9 **chill:** Kühle.
9f. **premonition:** Vorahnung.
11 **homely:** gemütlich, einfach.
13 **Drambuie:** schottischer Whiskylikör.
16 **hoax:** Streich, blinder Alarm.
16f. **fugitive:** flüchtig.
17 **odorless:** geruchlos.
18 **sarin:** chemischer Kampfstoff, Nervengas.

There was nothing, no Strauss, no crisp and efficient NPR correspondent delivering news of riots in Cincinnati and the imminent collapse of the infrastructure, no right-wing talk, no hip-hop, no jazz, no rock. I switched to AM, and after a painstaking search I hit on a weak signal that sounded as if it were coming from the bottom of Santa Monica Bay. *This is only a test*, a mechanical voice pronounced in what was now just the faintest whispering squeak, *in the event of an actual emergency please stay tuned to* ... and then it faded out. While I was fumbling to bring it back in, I happened upon a voice shouting something in Spanish. It was just a single voice, very agitated, rolling on tirelessly, and I listened in wonder and dread until the signal went dead just after midnight.

I didn't sleep that night. I'd begun to divine the magnitude of what was going on in the world below me – this was no hoax, no casual atrocity or ordinary attrition; this was the beginning of the end, the

1 **crisp:** knapp.
2 **NPR:** Abk. für *National Public Radio:* öffentlicher Radiosender.
3 **Cincinnati:** Großstadt im Bundesstaat Ohio.
imminent: unmittelbar bevorstehend, drohend.
5 **AM:** Abk. für *amplitude modulation:* Mittelwelle.
painstaking: gewissenhaft; mühsam.
7 **Santa Monica Bay:** Bucht und einer der wichtigsten Strände von Los Angeles.
9 **squeak:** Pieps.
14 **agitated:** aufgeregt.
17 **to divine:** erahnen, erspüren.
19 **atrocity:** Grausamkeit, Gräueltat.
20 **attrition:** Zermürbung.

Apocalypse, the utter failure and ultimate demise of all things human. I felt sick at heart. Lying there in the fastness of the cabin in the absolute and abiding dark of the wilderness, I was consumed with fear. I lay on my stomach and listened to the steady thunder of my heart pounding through the mattress, attuned to the slightest variation, waiting like a condemned man for the first harrowing sneeze.

Over the course of the next several days, the radio would sporadically come to life (I left it switched on at all times, day and night, as if I were going down in a sinking ship and could shout "Mayday!" into the receiver at the first stirring of a human voice). I'd be pacing the floor or spooning sugar into my tea or staring at a freshly inserted and eternally blank page in my ancient manual typewriter when the static would momentarily clear and a harried newscaster spoke out of the void to provide me with the odd and horrific detail: an oceanliner had run aground off

1 **demise:** Tod, Ableben.
3 **fastness:** Feste.
abiding: unvergänglich, bleibend.
4 **to be consumed with s.th.:** sich vor etwas verzehren.
6 **to pound:** hämmern, heftig klopfen.
6f. *(to be)* **attuned to s.th.** (fig.): auf etwas abgestimmt, an etwas gewöhnt sein.
8 **harrowing:** erschütternd, grauenhaft.
12 **Mayday:** internationaler Notruf im Funksprechverkehr.
16 **static:** atmosphärische Störungen, Rauschen.
17 **harried:** bedrängt.
newscaster: Nachrichtensprecher(in).
18 **void:** Leere.
19 **to run aground:** auflaufen, auf Grund laufen.

Cape Hatteras and nothing left aboard except three sleek and frisky cats and various puddles of flesh swathed in plaid shorts, polo shirts and sunglasses; no sound or signal had come out of South Florida in over thirty-six hours; a group of survivalists had seized Bill Gates' private jet in an attempt to escape to Antarctica, where it was thought the infection hadn't yet reached, but everyone aboard vomited black bile and died before the plane could leave the ground. Another announcer broke down in the middle of an unconfirmed report that every man, woman and child in Minneapolis was dead, and yet another came over the air early one morning shouting, "It kills! It kills! It kills in three days!" At that point, I jerked the plug out of the wall.

My first impulse, of course, was to help. To save Danielle, the frail and the weak, the young and the old, the chairman of the social studies department at the school where I teach (or taught), a student teacher with cropped red hair about whom I'd had several minutely detailed sexual fantasies. I even went

1 **Cape Hatteras:** Naturschutzgebiet an der Küste des Bundesstaats North Carolina; berüchtigter Schiffsfriedhof mit gefährlichen Strömungen und Sandbänken.
2 **sleek:** geschmeidig.
frisky: verspielt.
puddle: Pfütze.
3 **swathed:** eingewickelt, eingehüllt.
plaid: kariert.
12 **Minneapolis:** größte Stadt im Bundesstaat Minnesota mit 380 000 Einwohnern.
20 **cropped:** kurz geschnitten.

so far as to hike out to the road and take the car into Fish Fry Flats, but the bar/restaurant/gift shop/one-stop grocery/gas station was closed and locked and the parking lot deserted. I drove round the lot three times, debating whether I should continue on down the road or not, but then a lean furtive figure darted out of a shed at the corner of the lot and threw itself – himself – into the shadows beneath the deck of the main building. I recognized the figure immediately as the splay-footed and pony-tailed proprietor of the place, a man who would pump your gas with an inviting smile and then lure you into the gift shop to pay in the hope that the hand-carved Tule Indian figurines and Pen-Lite batteries would prove irresistible. I saw his feet protruding from beneath the deck, and they seemed to be jittering or trembling as if he were doing some sort of energetic new contra-dance that began in the prone position. For a long moment I sat

6 **furtive:** verstohlen.
to dart: flitzen.
8 **deck:** Terrasse.
10 **splay-footed:** spreizfüßig.
12 **to lure:** locken.
13 **hand-carved:** handgeschnitzt.
Tule Indian: 1873 wurde das Reservat für den Tule River Tribe of Yokut Indians in den Sierra-Nevada-Bergen Kaliforniens geschaffen; der Stamm lebt hauptsächlich vom Tourismus.
figurine: Figürchen.
14 **irresistible:** unwiderstehlich.
15 **to protrude:** herausragen, vorstehen.
16 **to jitter:** zittern.
17 **contra-dance:** Contredanse, Kontertanz.
18 **prone position:** Bauchlage.

there and watched those dancing feet, then I hit the lock button, rolled up the windows and drove back to the cabin.

What did I do? Ultimately? Nothing. Call it enlightened self-interest. Call it solipsism, self-preservation, cowardice, I don't care. I was terrified – who wouldn't be? – and I decided to stay put. I had plenty of food and firewood, fuel for the generator and propane for the stove, three reams of twenty-five percent cotton fiber bond, correction fluid, books, board games – Parcheesi and Monopoly – and a complete set of *National Geographic*, 1947–1962. (By way of explanation, I should mention that I am – or was – a social studies teacher at the Montecito School, a preparatory academy in a pricey suburb of Santa Barbara, and that the serendipity that spared me the fate of nearly all my fellow men and women was as simple and fortuitous a thing as a sabbatical leave. After fourteen years of unstinting service, I applied for and was granted a one-semester leave at half-salary for the purpose of writing a memoir of my deprived and

5 **solipsism:** Solipsismus, extreme Ichbezogenheit.
6 **cowardice:** Feigheit.
9 **ream:** Ries (480 oder 500 Blatt Papier); (coll.) große Menge.
10 **correction fluid:** Korrekturflüssigkeit.
11 **Parcheesi:** »Mensch, ärgere dich nicht« (Spiel).
14 **Montecito:** kleine Stadt bei Santa Barbara (Kalifornien).
15 **pricey:** teuer.
18 **fortuitous:** zufällig.
sabbatical leave: Forschungsurlaub.
19 **unstinting:** unermüdlich.
21 **deprived:** benachteiligt (Kind).

miserable Irish-Catholic upbringing. The previous year a high school teacher from New York – the name escapes me now – had enjoyed a spectacular *succès d'estime*, not to mention *d'argent*, with a memoir about his own miserable and deprived Irish-Catholic boyhood, and I felt I could profitably mine the same territory. And I got a good start on it too, until the plague hit. Now I ask myself what's the use – the publishers are all dead. Ditto the editors, agents, reviewers, booksellers and the great congenial book-buying public itself. What's the sense of writing? What's the sense of anything?)

At any rate, I stuck close to the cabin, writing at the kitchen table through the mornings, staring out the window into the ankles of the pines and redwoods as I summoned degrading memories of my alcoholic mother, father, aunts, uncles, cousins and grandparents, and in the afternoons I hiked up to the highest peak and looked down on the deceptive tranquillity of the San Joaquin Valley spread out like a continent below me. There were no planes in the sky

1 **upbringing:** Erziehung.
3 f. **succès d'estime ... d'argent** (Fr.): Achtungserfolg, um nicht zu sagen finanziellen Erfolg.
6 f. **to mine the same territory:** aus demselben Stoff Kapital schlagen.
9 **ditto:** ebenso.
10 **congenial:** geistesverwandt.
15 **redwood:** Mammutbaum.
16 **degrading:** erniedrigend.
19 **deceptive:** trügerisch.
19 f. **tranquillity:** Stille, Friedlichkeit.
20 **San Joaquin Valley:** fruchtbares Tal in Kalifornien, auch »Golden Valley« genannt.

overhead, no sign of traffic or movement anywhere, no sounds but the calling of the birds and the soughing of the trees as the breeze sifted through them. I stayed up there past dark one night and felt as serene and terrible as a god when I looked down at the velvet expanse of the world and saw no ray or glimmer of light. I plugged the radio back in that night, just to hear the fading comfort of man-made noise, of the static that emanates from nowhere and nothing. Because there was nothing out there, not anymore.

It was four weeks later – just about the time I was to have ended my hermitage and enjoyed the promised visit from Danielle – that I had my first human contact of the new age. I was at the kitchen window, beating powdered eggs into a froth for dinner, one ear half-attuned to the perfect and unbroken static hum of the radio, when there was a heavy thump on the deteriorating planks of the front deck. My first thought was that a branch had dropped out of the Jeffrey pine – or worse, that a bear had got wind of the

2f. **soughing:** Rauschen.
3 **to sift through s.th.:** etwas durchsieben.
4 **serene:** gelassen, ruhig.
5f. **velvet:** Samt; samtig.
6 **expanse:** weite Fläche.
9 **to emanate:** ausstrahlen.
12 **hermitage:** Einsiedelei.
15 **froth:** Schaum.
16 **hum:** Summen.
17 **thump:** dumpfer Schlag.
18 **deteriorating:** verfallen, morsch.
plank: Holzbrett.

corned beef hash I'd opened to complement the powdered eggs – but I was mistaken on both counts. The thump was still reverberating through the floorboards when I was surprised to hear a moan and then a curse – a distinctly human curse. "Oh, shit-fuck!" a woman's voice cried. "Open the goddamned door! Help, for shit's sake, help!"

I've always been a cautious animal. This may be one of my great failings, as my mother and later my fraternity brothers were always quick to point out, but on the other hand, it may be my greatest virtue. It's kept me alive when the rest of humanity has gone on to a quick and brutal extinction, and it didn't fail me in that moment. The door was locked. Once I'd got wind of what was going on in the world, though I was devastated and the thought of the radical transformation of everything I'd ever known gnawed at me day and night, I took to locking it against just such an eventuality as this. "Shit!" the voice raged. "I can hear you in there, you son of a bitch – I can *smell* you!"

I stood perfectly still and held my breath. The static breathed dismally through the speakers and I wished

1 **hash:** Haschee.
to complement: ergänzen, abrunden.
2 **on both counts:** in beiden Punkten.
3 **to reverberate:** widerhallen.
4 **moan:** Stöhnen.
10 **fraternity brother:** Mitglied einer Verbindung oder Vereinigung.
16 **devastated:** erschüttert.
17 **to gnaw at s.o.** (fig.): an jdm. nagen, jdn. quälen.
20 **son of a bitch** (vulg.): Saukerl.
22 **dismally** (adv.): trostlos.

I'd had the sense to disconnect the radio long ago. I stared down at the half-beaten eggs.

"I'm dying out here!" the voice cried. "I'm starving to death – hey, are you deaf in there or what? I said, I'm *starving*!"

And now of course I was faced with a moral dilemma. Here was a fellow human being in need of help, a member of a species whose value had just vaulted into the rarefied atmosphere occupied by the gnatcatcher, the condor and the beluga whale by virtue of its rarity. Help her? Of course I would help her. But at the same time, I knew if I opened that door I would invite the pestilence in and that three days hence both she and I would be reduced to our mortal remains.

"Open up!" she demanded, and the tattoo of her fists was the thunder of doom on the thin planks of the door.

It occurred to me suddenly that she couldn't be infected – she'd have been dead and wasted by now if she were. Maybe she was like me, maybe she'd been out brooding in her own cabin or hiking the mountain trails, utterly oblivious and immune to the general ca-

9 **to vault:** einen Sprung machen.
rarefied: dünn.
10 **gnatcatcher:** Mückenschnäpper (amerikanischer Singvogel).
13 **pestilence:** Pest.
16 **tattoo:** Trommeln, Trommelwirbel.
17 **doom:** Schicksal, Verhängnis.
22 **to brood:** grübeln.
23 **oblivious:** unwissend.
23f. **calamity:** Katastrophe.

lamity. Maybe she was beautiful, nubile, a new Eve for a new age, maybe she would fill my nights with passion and my days with joy. As if in a trance, I crossed the room and stood at the door, my fingers on the long brass stem of the bolt. "Are you alone?" I said, and the rasp of my own voice, so long in disuse, sounded strange in my ears.

I heard her draw in a breath of astonishment and outrage from the far side of the thin panel that separated us. "What the hell do you think, you son of a bitch? I've been lost out here in these stinking woods for I don't know how long and I haven't had a scrap for days, not a goddamn scrap, not even bark or grass or a handful of soggy trail mix. *Now will you fucking open this door?!*"

Still, I hesitated.

A rending sound came to me then, a sound that tore me open as surely as a surgical knife, from my groin to my throat: she was sobbing. Gagging for breath, and sobbing. "A frog," she sobbed, "I ate a goddamn slimy little putrid *frog*!"

1 **nubile:** attraktiv, gut entwickelt.
6 **rasp:** Krächzen.
9 **outrage:** Empörung.
panel: (Tür-)Paneel.
12 **scrap:** Bissen.
14 **soggy:** durchnässt.
17 **to rend:** zerreißen.
18 **surgical knife:** Operationsmesser.
19 **groin:** Leiste(ngegend).
to sob: schluchzen.
to gag: würgen.
21 **putrid:** verfault.

God help me. God save and preserve me. I opened the door.

Sarai was thirty-eight years old – that is, three years older than I – and she was no beauty. Not on the surface, anyway. Even if you discounted the twenty-odd pounds she'd lost and her hair that was like some crushed rodent's pelt and the cuts and bites and suppurating sores that made her skin look like a leper's, and tried, by a powerful leap of the imagination, to see her as she once might have been, safely ensconced in her condo in Tarzana and surrounded by all the accoutrements of feminine hygiene and beauty, she still wasn't much.

This was her story: she and her live-in boyfriend, Howard, were nature enthusiasts – at least Howard was, anyway – and just before the plague hit they'd set out to hike an interlocking series of trails in the Golden Trout Wilderness. They were well provisioned, with the best of everything – Howard managed a sporting goods store – and for the first three weeks

5 f. **twenty-odd pounds** (coll.): ungefähr zwanzig Pfund.
7 **rodent:** Nagetier.
pelt: Fell, Pelz.
7 f. **suppurating sores:** eiternde Wunden.
8 **leper:** Leprakranke(r).
10 f. **ensconced:** niedergelassen.
11 **condo:** Abk. für *condominium:* Eigentumswohnung.
Tarzana: Stadt in Kalifornien.
12 **accoutrements** (pl.): Ausrüstung.
17 **interlocking:** vernetzt, ineinander greifend.
18 **Golden Trout Wilderness:** Nationalpark in Kalifornien, benannt nach den typischen Fischen des Gebiets, den Goldforellen.

everything went according to plan. They ate delicious freeze-dried fettuccine Alfredo and shrimp couscous, drank cognac from a bota bag and made love wrapped in propylene, Gore-Tex and nylon. Mosquitoes and horseflies sampled her legs, but she felt good, born again, liberated from the traffic and the smog and her miserable desk in a miserable corner of the electronics company her father had founded. Then one morning, when they were camped by a stream, Howard went off with his day pack and a fly rod and never came back. She waited. She searched. She screamed herself hoarse. A week went by. Every day she searched in a new direction, following the stream both ways and combing every tiny rill and tributary, until finally she got herself lost. All streams were one stream, all hills and ridges alike. She had three Kudos bars with her and a six-ounce bag of peanuts, but no shelter and no freeze-dried entrées – all that was back at the camp she and Howard had made in happier times. A cold rain fell. There were no stars that night, and when something moved in the brush beside her she panicked and ran blindly

3 **bota bag:** (spanischer) Weinbeutel.
5 **horsefly:** Pferdebremse.
to sample: kosten, probieren.
10f. **fly rod:** Angelrute für die Fliegenfischerei.
12 **hoarse:** heiser.
14 **rill:** Bächlein.
15 **tributary:** Nebenfluss.
16 **ridge:** Bergkamm.
17 **Kudos bar:** bekannter amerikanischer Schokoriegel.
18 **entrée:** Hauptgericht.

through the dark, hammering her shins and destroying her face, her hair and her clothes. She'd been wandering ever since.

I made her a package of Top Ramen, gave her a towel and a bar of soap and showed her the primitive shover I'd rigged up above the ancient slab of the tub. I was afraid to touch her or even come too close to her. Sure I was skittish. Who wouldn't be when ninety-nine percent of the human race had just died off on the tailwind of a simple sneeze? Besides, I'd begun to adopt all the habits of the hermit – talking to myself, performing elaborate rituals over my felicitous stock of foodstuffs, dredging bursts of elementary school songs and beer jingles out of the depths of my impacted brain – and I resented having my space invaded. *Still.* Still, though, I felt that Sarai had been delivered to me by some higher power and that she'd been blessed in the way that I was – we'd escaped the infection. We'd survived. And we weren't just errant members of a selfish, suspicious and fragmented so-

1 **shin:** Schienbein.
4 **Top Ramen:** bekannte amerikanische Trockenfertiggerichte mit Nudeln.
6 **to rig s.th. up:** etwas aufbauen, improvisieren.
slab: Platte.
8 **skittish:** übermütig.
10 **tailwind:** Rückenwind.
11 **hermit:** Einsiedler.
12f. **felicitous:** glücklich.
13 **to dredge:** (fig.) ausgraben.
15 **impacted:** angeschlagen.
to resent s.th.: etwas übel nehmen.
19 **errant:** abtrünnig.

ciety, but the very foundation of a new one. She was a woman. I was a man.

At first, she wouldn't believe me when I waved a dismissive hand at the ridge behind the cabin and all that lay beyond it and informed her that the world was depeopled, that the Apocalypse had come and that she and I were among the solitary survivors – and who could blame her? As she sipped my soup and ate my flapjacks and treated her cuts and abrasions with my Neosporin and her hair with my shampoo, she must have thought she'd found a lunatic as her savior. "If you don't believe me," I said, and I was gloating, I was, sick as it may seem, "try the radio."

She looked up at me out of the leery brooding eyes of the one sane woman in a madhouse of impostors, plugged the cord in the socket and calibrated the dial as meticulously as a safecracker. She was rewarded by static – no dynamics even, just a single dull continu-

4 **dismissive:** abweisend.
6 **depeopled:** entvölkert.
7 **solitary:** einsam.
9 **flapjack:** Pfannkuchen.
9f. **abrasion:** Hautabschürfung.
10 **Neosporin:** antiseptische Salbe.
11 **lunatic:** Wahnsinnige(r).
13 **to gloat:** sich großtun, sich brüsten.
15 **leery:** misstrauisch.
16 **sane:** normal, geistig gesund.
madhouse (coll.): Irrenhaus.
impostor: Betrüger(in).
17 **to calibrate:** kalibrieren.
18 **meticulously** (adv.): sorgfältig, peinlich genau.

um – but she glared up at me as if I'd rigged the thing to disappoint her. "*So*," she spat, skinny as a refugee, her hair kinked and puffed up with my shampoo till it devoured her parsimonious and disbelieving little sliver of a face, "that doesn't prove a thing. It's broken, that's all."

When she got her strength back, we hiked out to the car and drove into Fish Fry Flats so she could see for herself. I was half-crazy with the terrible weight of the knowledge I'd been forced to hold inside me, and I can't describe the irritation I felt at her utter lack of interest – she treated me like a street gibberer, a psychotic, Cassandra in long pants. She condescended to me. She was *humoring* me, for God's sake, and the whole world lay in ruins around us. But she would have a rude awakening, she would, and the thought of it was what kept me from saying something I'd regret – I didn't want to lose my temper and scare her off, but I hate stupidity and willfulness. It's the one thing I won't tolerate in my students. Or wouldn't. Or didn't.

Fish Fry Flats, which in the best of times could hardly be mistaken for a metropolis, looked now as if

1 **to glare:** finster, zornig blicken.
to rig s.th.: etwas manipulieren.
3 **kinked:** gewellt.
4 **to devour:** verschlingen.
parsimonious: geizig.
5 **sliver:** Scheibchen.
12 **gibberer:** Idiot.
13 **Cassandra in long pants:** (eine) männliche Kassandra (die Warnerin in der Sage vom Trojanischen Krieg).
13f. **to condescend to s.o.:** jdn. herablassend behandeln.
14 **to humor s.o.:** jdn. dulden.

it had been deserted for a decade. Weeds had begun to sprout up through invisible cracks in the pavement, dust had settled over the idle gas pumps and the windows of the main building were etched with grime. And the animals – the animals were everywhere, marmots waddling across the lot as if they owned it, a pair of coyotes asleep in the shade of an abandoned pickup, ravens cawing and squirrels chittering. I cut the engine just as a bear the color of cinnamon toast tumbled stupendously through an already shattered window and lay on his back, waving his bloodied paws in the air as if he were drunk, which he was. As we discovered a few minutes later – once he'd lurched to his feet and staggered off into the bushes – a whole host of creatures had raided the grocery, stripping the candy display right down to the twisted wire rack, scattering Triscuits and Doritos, shattering jars of jam and jugs of port wine and grinding the hand-carved

2 **to sprout up:** sprießen.
4 **etched with grime:** von Schmutz überzogen.
5 f. **marmot:** Murmeltier.
6 **to waddle:** watscheln.
8 **to caw:** krächzen.
to chitter: schnattern.
9 **cinnamon:** Zimt.
10 **to tumble:** purzeln.
stupendously (adv.): fantastisch.
shattered: zersplittert.
13 f. **to lurch to one's feet:** sich aufrappeln.
14 **to stagger:** torkeln.
15 **host:** Menge, Masse.
17 **Triscuits:** Kräcker.
Doritos: Chips.
18 f. **to grind s.th. underfoot:** auf etwas herumtrampeln.

Tule Indian figurines underfoot. There was no sign of the formerly sunny proprietor or of his dancing feet – I could only imagine that the ravens, coyotes and ants had done their work.

But Sarai – she was still an unbeliever, even after she dropped a quarter into the public telephone and put the dead black plastic receiver to her ear. For all the good it did her, she might as well have tried coaxing a dial tone out of a stone or a block of wood, and I told her so. She gave me a sour look, the sticks of her bones briefly animated beneath a sweater and jacket I'd loaned her – it was the end of October and getting cold at seventy-two hundred feet – and then she tried another quarter, and then another, before she slammed the receiver down in a rage and turned her seething face on me. "The lines are down, that's all," she sneered. And then her mantra: "It doesn't prove a thing."

While she'd been frustrating herself, I'd been loading the car with canned goods, after entering the main building through the broken window and unlatching the door from the inside. "And what about all this?" I said, irritated, hot with it, sick to death of her and her thick-headedness. I gestured at the bloated and lazy coyotes, the hump in the bushes that was the drunken

3 **ant:** Ameise.
8f. **to coax:** hervorlocken.
16 **seething:** vor Wut schäumend.
17 **to sneer:** spotten.
21 **to unlatch:** entriegeln.
24 **bloated:** aufgedunsen.
25 **hump:** Hügel, Buckel.

bear, the waddling marmots and the proprietary ravens.

"I don't know," she said, clenching her jaws. "And I don't care." Her eyes had a dull sheen to them. They were insipid and bovine, exactly the color of the dirt at her feet. And her lips – thin and stingy, collapsed in a riot of vertical lines like a dried-up mud puddle. I hated her in that moment, godsend or no. Oh, how I hated her.

"What are you *doing*?" she demanded as I loaded the last of the groceries into the car, settled into the driver's seat and turned the engine over. She was ten feet from me, caught midway between the moribund phone booth and the living car. One of the coyotes lifted its head at the vehemence of her tone and gave her a sleepy, yellow-eyed look.

"Going back to the cabin," I said.

"You're *what*?" Her face was pained. She'd been through agonies. I was a devil and a madman.

"Listen, Sarai, it's all over. I've told you time and again. You don't have a job anymore. You don't have to pay rent, utility bills, don't have to make car pay-

1 **proprietary:** besitzergreifend.
3 **to clench one's jaws:** die Kiefer zusammenpressen.
4 **sheen:** Glanz.
5 **insipid:** ausdruckslos.
bovine (fig.): stupide, einfältig.
6 **stingy:** geizig, knauserig.
8 **godsend:** Geschenk des Himmels.
13 **moribund:** zum Aussterben verurteilt.
15 **vehemence:** Vehemenz, Heftigkeit.
19 **agony:** Todesqual.
22 **utility bills:** Strom-, Wasser- und Telefonrechnungen.

ments or remember your mother's birthday. It's over. Don't you get it?"

"You're insane! You're a shithead! I hate you!"

The engine was purring beneath my feet, fuel awasting, but there was infinite fuel now, and though I realized the gas pumps would no longer work, there were millions upon millions of cars and trucks out there in the world with full tanks to siphon, and no one around to protest. I could drive a Ferrari if I wanted, a Rolls, a Jag, anything. I could sleep on a bed of jewels, stuff the mattress with hundred-dollar bills, prance through the streets in a new pair of Italian loafers and throw them into the gutter each night and get a new pair in the morning. But I was afraid. Afraid of the infection, the silence, the bones rattling in the wind. "I know it," I said. "I'm insane. I'm a shithead. I admit it. But I'm going back to the cabin and you can do anything you want – it's a free country. Or at least it used to be."

I wanted to add that it was a free world now, a free universe, and that God was in the details, the biblical God, the God of famine, flood and pestilence, but I never got the chance. Before I could open my mouth

3 **insane:** wahnsinnig.
4 **to purr:** schnurren.
4f. **awasting:** verschwendend.
8 **to siphon:** absaugen.
12 **to prance:** herumhüpfen.
13 **loafer:** Halbschuh.
gutter: Gosse, Rinnstein.
15 **to rattle:** klappern.

she bent for a stone and heaved it into the windshield, splintering me with flecks and shards of safety glass. "Die!" she shrieked. "*You* die, you shit!"

That night we slept together for the first time. In the morning, we packed up a few things and drove down the snaking mountain road to the charnel house of the world.

I have to confess that I've never been much of a fan of the apocalyptic potboiler, the doomsday film shot through with special effects and asinine dialogue or the cyberpunk version of a grim and relentless future. What these entertainments had led us to expect – the roving gangs, the inhumanity, the ascendancy of machines and the redoubled pollution and ravaging of the earth – wasn't at all what it was like. There were no roving gangs – they were all dead, to a man, woman and tattooed punk – and the only machines still functioning were the automobiles and weed whippers and such that we the survivors chose to

1 **to heave:** hieven, wuchten, werfen, schmeißen.
2 **to splinter:** mit Splittern übersäen.
shard: Scherbe.
3 **to shriek:** kreischen.
6 **charnel house:** Leichenhalle.
9 **potboiler:** rein kommerzielles Werk.
doomsday: der Jüngste Tag.
10 **asinine:** idiotisch.
11 **relentless:** unerbittlich, erbarmungslos.
13 **to rove:** herumstromern, -streifen, vagabundieren.
ascendancy: Vormachtstellung.
14 **ravaging:** Verwüsten, Zerstörung.
18f. **weed whipper:** Unkrautentferner.

put into prosaic action. And a further irony was that the survivors were the least likely and least qualified to organize anything, either for better or worse. We were the fugitive, the misfit, the recluse, and we were so widely scattered we'd never come into contact with one another, anyway – and that was just the way we liked it. There wasn't even any looting of the supermarkets – there was no need. There was more than enough for everybody who ever was or would be.

Sarai and I drove down the mountain road, through the deserted small town of Springville and the deserted larger town of Porterville, and then we turned south for Bakersfield, the Grapevine and Southern California. She wanted to go back to her apartment, to Los Angeles, and see if her parents and her sisters were alive still – she became increasingly vociferous on that score as the reality of what had happened began to seep through to her – but I was driving and I wanted to avoid Los Angeles at all costs. To my mind, the place had been a pit before the scourge hit, and

1 **prosaic:** nüchtern.
4 **fugitive:** Flüchtling.
misfit: Außenseiter(in).
recluse: Einsiedler(in).
7 **looting:** Plündern.
12 ff. **Springville / Porterville / Bakersfield / the Grapevine:** kleinere Städte in Kalifornien.
17 **vociferous:** laut, lautstark.
19 **to seep through to s.o.:** (fig.) langsam zu jdm. durchsickern, jdm. langsam bewusst werden.
21 **scourge:** Bestrafung, Geißel.

now it was a pit heaped with seven million moldering corpses. She carped and moaned and whined and threatened, but she was in shock too and couldn't quite work herself up to her usual pitch, and so we turned west and north on Route 126 and headed toward Montecito, where for the past ten years I'd lived in a cottage on one of the big estates there – the DuPompier place, *Mírame*.

By the way, when I mentioned earlier that the freeways were clear, I was speaking metaphorically – they were free of traffic, but cluttered with abandoned vehicles of all sorts, take your pick, from gleaming choppers with thousand-dollar gold-fleck paint jobs to sensible family cars, Corvettes, Winnebagos, eighteen-wheelers and even fire engines and police cruisers. Twice, when Sarai became especially insistent, I pulled alongside one or another of these abandoned cars, swung open her door and said, "Go ahead. Take this Cadillac" – or BMW or whatever – "and drive yourself any damn place you please. Go on. What are you waiting for?" But her face shrank till it was as

1 **to molder:** vermodern, verwesen.
2 **corpse:** Leiche.
to carp: nörgeln.
to moan: stöhnen.
to whine: jammern.
7 **estate:** Grundstück.
11 **cluttered:** voll gestopft.
13 **chopper** (coll.): Maschine, Motorrad.
14 **Corvette:** teure Automarke (Chevrolet).
Winnebago: Wohnmobil-Marke.
16 **insistent:** hartnäckig.
21 **to shrink:** schrumpfen.

small as a doll's and her eyes went stony with fear: those cars were catacombs, each and every one of them, and the horror of that was more than anybody could bear.

So we drove on, through a preternatural silence and a world that already seemed primeval, up the Coast Highway and along the frothing bright boatless sea and into Montecito. It was evening when we arrived, and there wasn't a soul in sight. If it weren't for that – and a certain creeping untended look to the lawns, shrubs and trees – you wouldn't have noticed anything out of the ordinary. My cottage, built in the twenties of local sandstone and draped in wisteria till it was all but invisible, was exactly as I'd left it. We pulled into the silent drive with the great house looming in the near distance, a field of dark reflective glass that held the blood of the declining sun in it, and Sarai barely glanced up. Her thin shoulders were hunched and she was staring at a worn place on the mat between her feet.

"We're here," I announced, and I got out of the car.

2 **catacombs:** Katakomben.
5 **preternatural: 1.** übernatürlich; **2.** unnatürlich, außergewöhnlich, abnorm.
6 **primeval:** urzeitlich.
7 **to froth:** schäumen.
10 **creeping:** unheimlich.
untended: vernachlässigt, ungepflegt.
13 **draped:** gehüllt.
wisteria: Wisteria, Glyzine, Blauregen.
15 f. **to loom:** aufragen, -tauchen.
19 **hunched:** hochgezogen (Schultern).

She turned her eyes to me, stricken, suffering, a waif. “Where?”

“Home.”

It took her a moment, but when she responded she spoke slowly and carefully, as if she were just learning the language. “I have no home,” she said. “Not anymore.”

So. What to tell you? We didn’t last long, Sarai and I, though we were pioneers, though we were the last hope of the race, drawn together by the tenacious glue of fear and loneliness. I knew there wouldn’t be much opportunity for dating in the near future, but we just weren’t suited to each other. In fact, we were as unsuited as any two people could ever be, and our sex was tedious and obligatory, a ballet of mutual need and loathing, but to my mind at least, there was a bright side – here was the chance to go forth and be fruitful and do what we could to repopulate the vast and aching sphere of the planet. Within the month, however, Sarai had disabused me of that notion.

It was a silky, fog-hung morning, the day deepening around us, and we’d just gone through the mechanics

1 **stricken:** schmerzerfüllt, leidgeprüft.
2 **waif:** obdachloses Kind.
10 **tenacious:** hartnäckig.
15 **tedious:** langweilig, öde.
16 **loathing:** Abscheu.
18 **to repopulate:** wieder bevölkern.
19 **aching:** wund, schmerzend.
20 **to disabuse:** befreien.
notion: Gedanke, Vorstellung.

of sex and were lying exhausted and unsatisfied in the rumple of my gritty sheets (water was a problem and we did what laundry we could with what we were able to haul down from the estate's swimming pool). Sarai was breathing through her mouth, an irritating snort and burble that got on my nerves, but before I could say anything, she spoke in a hard shriveled little nugget of a voice. "You're no Howard," she said.

"Howard's dead," I said. "He deserted you."

She was staring at the ceiling. "Howard was gold," she mused in a languid, reflective voice, "and you're shit."

It was childish, I know, but the dig at my sexual performance really stung – not to mention the ingratitude of the woman – and I came back at her. "You came to me," I said. "I didn't ask for it – I was doing fine out there on the mountain without you. And where do you think you'd be now if it wasn't for me? Huh?"

She didn't answer right away, but I could feel her

2 **rumple:** zerknülltes Durcheinander.
gritty: sandig.
4 **to haul:** schleppen.
6 **snort:** Schnarchen.
burble: Gurgeln.
7 **shriveled:** zusammengeschrumpft.
8 **nugget:** Klumpen, Bröckchen.
12 **to muse:** sinnieren.
languid: träge, müde.
14f. **the dig at my sexual performance:** die spitze Bemerkung über meine Leistung beim Sex.
15f. **ingratitude:** Undankbarkeit.

consolidating in the bed beside me, magma becoming rock. "I'm not going to have sex with you again," she said, and still she was staring at the ceiling. "Ever. I'd rather use my finger."

"You're no Danielle," I said.

She sat up then, furious, all her ribs showing and her shrunken breasts clinging to the remains of them like an afterthought. "Fuck Danielle," she spat. "And fuck you."

I watched her dress in silence, but as she was lacing up her hiking boots I couldn't resist saying, "It's no joy for me either, Sarai, but there's a higher principle involved here than our likes and dislikes or any kind of animal gratification, and I think you know what I'm talking about –"

She was perched on the edge of a leather armchair I'd picked up at a yard sale years ago, when money and things had their own reality. She'd laced up the right boot and was working on the left, laces the color of rust, blunt white fingers with the nails bitten to the quick. Her mouth hung open slightly and I could see the pink tip of her tongue caught between her teeth as she worked mindlessly at her task, reverting like a

1 **to consolidate:** sich verhärten.
14 **gratification:** Befriedigung.
16 **to be perched:** hocken, thronen.
17 **yard sale:** Lagerverkauf.
20 **blunt:** stumpf, stummelig.
20f. **to bite one's nails to the quick:** die Fingernägel bis zum Fleisch abkauen.
23 **to revert:** zurückkehren.

child to her earliest training and her earliest habits. She gave me a blank look.

"Procreation, I mean. If you look at it in a certain way, it's – well, it's our duty."

Her laugh stung me. It was sharp and quick, like the thrust of a knife. "You idiot," she said, and she laughed again, showing the gold in her back teeth. "I hate children, always have – they're little monsters that grow up to be uptight fussy pricks like you." She paused, smiled, and released an audible breath. "I had my tubes tied fifteen years ago."

That night she moved into the big house, a replica of a Moorish castle in Seville, replete with turrets and battlements. The paintings and furnishings were exquisite, and there were some twelve thousand square feet of living space, graced with carved wooden ceilings, colored tiles, rectangular arches, a loggia and formal gardens. Nor had the DuPompiers spoiled the place by being so thoughtless as to succumb inside – they'd died, Julius, Eleanor and their daughter, Kelly,

3 **procreation:** Zeugung, Fortpflanzung.
6 **thrust:** Stoß.
9 **uptight fussy pricks** (vulg.): verklemmte kleinliche Arschlöcher.
10 **audible:** hörbar.
10f. **I had my tubes tied:** ich habe mich sterilisieren lassen (durch Ligation der Eileiter).
12 **replica:** Nachbildung.
13 **Moorish:** maurisch.
replete: ausgestattet.
turret: Eckturm.
14 **battlements:** Zinnen.
17 **tiles:** Fliesen.
19 **to succumb:** sich beugen, nachgeben.

under the arbor in back, the white bones of their hands eternally clasped. I wished Sarai good use of the place. I did. Because by that point I didn't care if she moved into the White House, so long as I didn't have to deal with her anymore.

Weeks slipped by. Months. Occasionally I would see the light of Sarai's Coleman lantern lingering in one of the high windows of *Mírame* as night fell over the coast, but essentially I was as solitary – and as lonely – as I'd been in the cabin in the mountains. The rains came and went. It was spring. Everywhere the untended gardens ran wild, the lawns became fields, the orchards forests, and I took to walking round the neighborhood with a baseball bat to ward off the packs of feral dogs for which Alpo would never again materialize in a neat bowl in the corner of a dry and warm kitchen. And then one afternoon, while I was at Von's, browsing the aisles for pasta, bottled marinara and Green Giant asparagus spears amid a scattering of rats and the lingering stench of the perished perish-

1 **arbor:** Laube.
2 **to clasp:** umklammern, verschränken; (Hände) falten.
7 **Coleman lantern:** Handelsname für Campinglaternen.
to linger: verharren.
14 **to ward off:** abwehren.
15 **feral:** verwildert.
Alpo: Handelsname für ein Hundefutter.
18 **to browse:** durchsuchen.
aisle: (Seiten-)Gang.
marinara: Marinade.
19 **asparagus spears:** Spargelspitzen.
20 **stench:** Gestank.
20 f. **perished perishables:** verdorbene verderbliche Waren.

ables, I detected movement at the far end of the next aisle over. My first thought was that it must be a dog or a coyote that had somehow managed to get in to feed on the rats or the big twenty-five-pound bags of Purina Dog Chow, but then, with a shock, I realized I wasn't alone in the store.

In all the time I'd been coming here for groceries, I'd never seen a soul, not even Sarai or one of the six or seven other survivors who were out there occupying the mansions in the hills. Every once in a while I'd see lights shining in the wall of the night – someone had even managed to fire up a generator at Las Tejas, a big Italianate villa half a mile away – and every so often a car would go helling up the distant freeway, but basically we survivors were shy of one another and kept to ourselves. It was fear, of course, the little spark of panic that told you the contagion was abroad again and that the best way to avoid it was to avoid all human contact. So we did. Strenuously.

But I couldn't ignore the squeak and rattle of a shopping cart wheeling up the bottled water aisle, and when I turned the corner, there she was, Felicia, with her flowing hair and her scared and sorry eyes. I didn't know her name then, not at first, but I recognized her – she was one of the tellers at the Bank of

5 **Purina Dog Chow:** Handelsname für ein Hundefutter.
10 **mansion:** Villa.
17 **contagion:** Seuche.
19 **strenuously** (adv.): entschieden, energisch.
20 **squeak:** Quietschen.
rattle: Klappern.
25 **teller:** Kassierer(in).

America branch where I cashed my checks. Formerly cashed them, that is. My first impulse was to back wordlessly away, but I mastered it – how could I be afraid of what was human, so palpably human, and appealing? "Hello," I said, to break the tension, and then I was going to say something stupid like "I see you made it too" or "Tough times, huh?" but instead I settled for "Remember me?"

She looked stricken. Looked as if she were about to bolt – or die on the spot. But her lips were brave and they came together and uttered my name. "Mr. Halloran?" she said, and it was so ordinary, so plebeian, so real.

I smiled and nodded. My name is – was – Francis Xavier Halloran III, a name I've hated since Tyrone Johnson (now presumably dead) tormented me with it in kindergarten, chanting "Francis, Francis, Francis" till I wanted to sink through the floor. But it was a new world now, a world burgeoning and bursting at the seams to discover the lineaments of its new forms and rituals. "Call me Jed," I said.

Nothing happens overnight, especially not in plague times. We were wary of each other, and every

4 **palpably** (adv.): eindeutig, spürbar.
10 **to bolt:** Reißaus nehmen.
12f. **plebeian:** plebejisch, primitiv.
17 **to chant:** skandieren.
19 **burgeoning:** hoffnungsvoll, expandierend.
20 **seam:** Naht.
lineaments: Grundzüge.
23 **to be wary of s.o.:** sich vor jdm. in Acht nehmen.

banal phrase and stultifying cliché of the small talk we made as I helped her load her groceries into the back of her Range Rover reverberated hugely with the absence of all the multitudes who'd used those phrases before us. Still, I got her address that afternoon – she'd moved into Villa Ruscello, a mammoth place set against the mountains, with a creek, pond and Jacuzzi for fresh water – and I picked her up two nights later in a Rolls Silver Cloud and took her to my favorite French restaurant. The place was untouched and pristine, with a sweeping view of the sea, and I lit some candles and poured us each a glass of twenty-year-old Bordeaux, after which we feasted on canned crab, truffles, cashews and marinated artichoke hearts.

I'd like to tell you that she was beautiful, because that's the way it should be, the way of the fable and the fairy tale, but she wasn't – or not conventionally, anyway. She was a little heavier than she might have been ideally, but that was a relief after stringy Sarai, and her eyes were ever so slightly crossed. Yet she was decent and kind, sweet even, and more important, she was available.

We took walks together, raided overgrown gardens for lettuce, tomatoes and zucchini, planted strawber-

1 **stultifying:** (fig.) lähmend.
3 **to reverberate:** widerhallen.
6 **mammoth:** riesig, gigantisch.
7 **creek:** Bachlauf.
8 **Jacuzzi:** Whirlpool.
11 **pristine:** unberührt, makellos.
20 **stringy:** groß und dünn.

ries and snow peas in the middle of the waist-high lawn at Villa Ruscello. One day we drove to the mountains and brought back the generator so we could have lights and refrigeration in the cottage – ice cubes, now there was a luxury – and begin to work our way through the eight thousand titles at the local video store. It was nearly a month before anything happened between us – anything sexual, that is. And when it did, she first felt obligated, out of a sense of survivor's guilt, I suppose, to explain to me how she came to be alive and breathing still when everyone she'd ever known had vanished off the face of the earth. We were in the beamed living room of my cottage, sharing a bottle of Dom Pérignon 1970, with the three-hundred-ten-dollar price tag still on it, and I'd started a fire against the gathering night and the wet raw smell of rain on the air. "You're going to think I'm an idiot," she said.

I made a noise of demurral and put my arm round her.

"Did you ever hear of a sensory deprivation tank?"

1 **snow peas:** Zuckerschoten.
9 **to feel obligated:** sich verpflichtet fühlen.
13 **beamed:** mit Holzbalkendecke.
19 **demurral:** Einwand.
21 **sensory deprivation tank:** Sinnesreiz-Entzugstank, Isolationstank; 1954 von John C. Lilly entwickelter, gegen Licht und Geräusche abgeschotteter Raum, der das Erreichen meditativer Zustände fördern soll. Im Inneren der dunklen, schalldichten Kabine befindet sich eine Art Badewanne mit warmem Salzwasser. Die Salzkonzentration ist so hoch, dass die darin badenden Personen im Wasser schweben und das Gefühl für die eigenen Körpergrenzen verlieren.

She was peering up at me through the scrim of her hair, gold and red highlights, health in a bottle.

"Yeah, sure," I said. "But you don't mean –?"

"It was an older one, a model that's not on the market anymore – one of the originals. My roommate's sister – Julie Angier? – she had it out in her garage on Padaro, and she was really into it. You could get in touch with your inner self, relax, maybe even have an out-of-body experience, that's what she said, and I figured why not?" She gave me a look, shy and passionate at once, to let me know that she was the kind of girl who took experience seriously. "They put salt water in it, three hundred gallons, heated to your body temperature, and then they shut the lid on you and there's nothing, absolutely nothing there – it's like going to outer space. Or inner space. Inside yourself."

"And you were in there when –?"

She nodded. There was something in her eyes I couldn't read – pride, triumph, embarrassment, a spark of sheer lunacy. I gave her an encouraging smile.

"For days, I guess," she said. "I just sort of lost track of everything, who I was, where I was – you know? And I didn't wake up till the water started getting cold" – she looked at her feet – "which I guess is

1 **to peer:** starren, schielen.
scrim: (Haar-)Schleier.
19 **to nod:** nicken.
21 **spark:** Funke.
lunacy: Wahnsinn.

when the electricity went out because there was nobody left to run the power plants. And then I pushed open the lid and the sunlight through the window was like an atom bomb, and then, then I called out Julie's name, and she … well, she never answered."

Her voice died in her throat and she turned those sorrowful eyes on me. I put my other arm around her and held her. "Hush," I whispered, "it's all right now, everything's all right." It was a conventional thing to say, and it was a lie, but I said it, and I held her and felt her relax in my arms.

It was then, almost to the precise moment, that Sarai's naked sliver of a face appeared at the window, framed by her two uplifted hands and a rock the size of my Webster's unabridged. "What about *me*, you son of a bitch!" she shouted, and there it was again, everlasting stone and frangible glass, and not a glazier left alive on the planet.

I wanted to kill her. It was amazing – three people I knew of had survived the end of everything, and it was one too many. I felt vengeful. Biblical. I felt like storming Sarai's ostentatious castle and wringing her chicken neck for her, and I think I might have if it

7 **sorrowful:** traurig.
15 **Webster's unabridged:** ungekürztes Wörterbuch von Webster, benannt nach dem amerikanischen Lexikographen Noah Webster (1758–1843).
17 **frangible:** zerbrechlich.
glazier: Glaser.
21 **vengeful:** rachsüchtig.
22 **ostentatious:** pompös, protzig.

weren't for Felicia. "Don't let her spoil it for us," she murmured, the gentle pressure of her fingers on the back of my neck suddenly holding my full attention, and we went into the bedroom and closed the door on all that mess of emotion and glass.

In the morning, I stepped into the living room and was outraged all over again. I cursed and stomped and made a fool of myself over heaving the rock back through the window and attacking the shattered glass as if it were alive – I admit I was upset out of all proportion to the crime. This was a new world, a new beginning, and Sarai's nastiness and negativity had no place in it. Christ, there were only three of us – couldn't we get along?

Felicia had repaired dozens of windows in her time. Her little brothers (dead now) and her fiancé (dead too) were forever throwing balls around the house, and she assured me that a shattered window was nothing to get upset over (though she bit her lip and let her eyes fill at the mention of her fiancé, and who could blame her?). So we consulted the Yellow Pages, drove to the nearest window glass shop and broke in as gently as possible. Within the hour, the new pane had been installed and the putty was drying in the sun, and watching Felicia at work had so elevated my spirits I suggested a little shopping spree to celebrate.

7 **outraged:** empört.
to stomp: aufstampfen.
12 **nastiness:** Gemeinheit, Bosheit.
23 **pane:** Glasscheibe.
24 **putty:** Kitt.
26 **shopping spree:** Einkaufsbummel.

"Celebrate what?" She was wearing a No Fear T-shirt and an Anaheim Angels cap and there was a smudge of off-white putty on her chin.

"You," I said. "The simple miracle of you."

And that was fine. We parked on the deserted streets of downtown Santa Barbara and had the stores to ourselves – clothes, the latest (and last) best-sellers, CDs, a new disc player to go with our newly electrified house. Others had visited some of the stores before us, of course, but they'd been polite and neat about it, almost as if they were afraid to betray their presence, and they always closed the door behind them. We saw deer feeding in the courtyards and one magnificent tawny mountain lion stalking the wrong way up a one-way street. By the time we got home, I was elated. Everything was going to work out, I was sure of it.

The mood didn't last long. As I swung into the drive, the first thing I saw was the yawning gap where the new window had been, and beyond it, the undifferentiated heap of rubble that used to be my living room. Sarai had been back. And this time she'd done a thorough job, smashing lamps and pot-

2 **Anaheim Angels** (pl.): Football-Mannschaft aus Los Angeles.
3 **smudge:** Fleck.
11 **to betray:** verraten.
14 **tawny:** gelbbraun.
mountain lion: Puma.
to stalk: pirschen.
16 **elated:** begeistert.
21 **rubble:** Schutt, Trümmer.
23 f. **pottery:** Töpferware; Geschirr.

tery, poking holes in our cans of beef stew and chili con carne, scattering coffee, flour and sugar all over everything and dumping sand in the generator's fuel tank. Worst of all, she'd taken half a dozen pairs of Felicia's panties and nailed them to the living room wall, a crude *X* slashed across the crotch of each pair. It was hateful and savage – human, that's what it was, human – and it killed all the joy we'd taken in the afternoon and the animals and the infinite and various riches of the mall. Sarai had turned it all to shit.

"We'll move to my place," Felicia said. "Or any place you want. How about an oceanfront house – didn't you say you'd always wanted to live right on the ocean?"

I had. But I didn't want to admit it. I stood in the middle of the desecrated kitchen and clenched my fists. "I don't want any other place. This is my home. I've lived here for ten years and I'll be damned if I'm going to let *her* drive me out."

It was an irrational attitude – again, childish – and Felicia convinced me to pack up a few personal items (my high school yearbook, my reggae albums, a signed first edition of *For Whom the Bell Tolls*, a pair of deer antlers I'd found in the woods when I was

1 **to poke:** stechen, bohren.
6 **to slash:** schlitzen.
crotch: Schritt, Zwickel.
16 **desecrated:** geschändet, entweiht.
16f. **to clench one's fists:** die Fäuste ballen.
23 **"For Whom the Bell Tolls":** Roman von Ernest Hemingway (1898–1961), veröffentlicht 1940.
24 **antlers** (pl.): Geweih.

eight) and move into a place on the ocean for a few days. We drove along the coast road at a slow, stately pace, looking over this house or that, until we finally settled on a grand modern place that was all angles and glass and broad sprawling decks. I got lucky and caught a few perch in the surf, and we barbecued them on the beach and watched the sun sink into the western bluffs.

The next few days were idyllic, and we thought about little beyond love and food and the way the water felt on our skin at one hour of the day or another, but still, the question of Sarai nagged at me. I was reminded of her every time I wanted a cold drink, for instance, or when the sun set and we had to make do with candles and kerosene lanterns – we'd have to go out and dig up another generator, we knew that, but they weren't exactly in demand in a place like Santa Barbara (in the old days, that is) and we didn't know where to look. And so yes, I couldn't shake the image of Sarai and the look on her face and the things she'd said and done. And I missed my house, because I'm a creature of habit, like anybody else. Or more so. Definitely more so.

Anyway, the solution came to us a week later, and it came in human form – at least it appeared in human form, but it was a miracle and no doubt about it.

2 **stately:** würdevoll, gemessen.
5 **sprawling:** großflächig.
6 **perch:** Barsch(e).
8 **bluff:** Kliff.
12 **to nag at s.o.:** jdm. keine Ruhe lassen.

Felicia and I were both on the beach – naked, of course, as naked and without shame or knowledge of it as Eve and Adam – when we saw a figure marching resolutely up the long curving finger of sand that stretched away into the haze of infinity. As the figure drew closer, we saw that it was a man, a man with a scraggly salt-and-pepper beard and hair the same color trailing away from a bald spot worn into his crown. He was dressed in hiking clothes, big-grid boots, a bright blue pack riding his back like a second set of shoulders. We stood there, naked, and greeted him.

"Hello," he said, stopping a few feet from us and staring first at my face, then at Felicia's breasts, and finally, with an effort, bending to check the laces of his boots. "Glad to see you two made it," he said, speaking to the sand.

"Likewise," I returned.

Over lunch on the deck – shrimp salad sandwiches on Felicia-baked bread – we traded stories. It seems he was hiking in the mountains when the pestilence descended – "The mountains?" I interrupted. "Whereabouts?"

"Oh," he said, waving a dismissive hand, "up in the

5 **haze:** Dunst.
infinity: Unendlichkeit.
7 **scraggly:** zottelig.
salt-and-pepper: meliert.
8 **to trail away:** in Strähnen herabhängen.
9 **crown:** Scheitel.
big-grid: mit gepolstertem Fußbett.
22 **to descend:** einfallen, heimsuchen.

Sierras, just above this little town – you've probably never heard of it – Fish Fry Flats?"

I let him go on a while, explaining how he'd lost his girlfriend and wandered for days before he finally came out on a mountain road and appropriated a car to go on down to Los Angeles – "One big cemetery" – and how he'd come up the coast and had been wandering ever since. I don't think I've ever felt such exhilaration, such a rush of excitement, such perfect and inimitable a sense of closure.

I couldn't keep from interrupting him again. "I'm clairvoyant," I said, raising my glass to the man sitting opposite me, to Felicia and her breasts, to the happy fishes in the teeming seas and the birds flocking without number in the unencumbered skies. "Your name's Howard, right?"

Howard was stunned. He set down his sandwich and wiped a fleck of mayonnaise from his lips. "How did you guess?" he said, gaping up at me out of eyes that were innocent and pure, the newest eyes in the world.

I just smiled and shrugged, as if it were my secret. "After lunch," I said, "I've got somebody I want you to meet."

8 f. **exhilaration:** Hochgefühl.
10 **inimitable:** einzigartig.
11 f. **to be clairvoyant:** hellsehen können.
14 **to teem:** wimmeln.
15 **unencumbered:** unbelastet.
17 **stunned:** wie betäubt, überwältigt.
19 **to gape up at s.o.:** jdn. mit offenem Mund anstarren.
22 **to shrug:** die Achseln zucken.

Peep Hall

I like my privacy. My phone is unlisted, my mailbox locks with a key, and the gate across the driveway automatically shuts behind me when I pull in. I've got my own little half-acre plot in the heart of this sunny little university town, and it's fenced all the way round. The house is a Craftsman-era bungalow, built in 1910, and the yard is lush with mature foliage, including the two grand old oaks that screen me from the street out front, a tsunami of Bougainvillea that long ago swallowed up the chainlink on both sides of the place, half a dozen tree ferns in the fifteen-foot range, and a whole damp, sweet-earth-smelling forest of Pittosporum, acacia, and blue gum eucalyptus crowding out what's left of the lawn.

1 **to peep:** lugen, spähen.
2 **my phone is unlisted:** ich habe eine Geheimnummer.
7 **Craftsman-era:** architektonischer Stil, beliebt am Anfang des 20. Jh.s besonders in Kalifornien.
8 **lush:** üppig.
foliage: Laubwerk, Blätter.
10 **Bougainvillea:** tropischer und subtropischer Strauch oder kleiner Baum mit zahlreichen kräftig-violetten Blüten.
11 **chainlink:** Maschendraht(zaun).
12 **tree fern:** Baumfarn.
14 **Pittosporum:** Klebsame; bis 25 m hoher, immergrüner Baum oder Strauch mit spitzen Blättern.
acacia: Akazie.

When I sit on the porch in the afternoon, all I see is twenty shades of green, and when someone bicycles by or the couple across the way get into one of their biweekly wrangles, I'm completely invisible, though I'm sitting right here with my feet propped up, taking it all in. I haven't been to a concert or a sporting event for as long as I can remember, or even a play or the movies, because crowds irritate me, all that jostling and hooting, the bad breath, the evil looks, not to mention the microbes hanging over all those massed heads like bad money on a bad bet. And no, I'm not a crank. I'm not crazy. And I'm not old, or not particularly (I'll be forty-one in November). But I do like my privacy, and I don't think there's any crime in that, especially when you work as hard as I do. Once I pull my car into the driveway, I just want to be left alone.

Six nights a week, and two afternoons, I stir *Mojitos* and shake martinis at the El Encanto Hotel, where I wear a bowtie and a frozen smile. I don't have any pets, I don't like walking, my parents are dead, and my wife – my *ex*-wife – may as well be. When I'm not

1 **porch:** Veranda.
4 **biweekly wrangles:** Streitigkeiten, die zweimal in der Woche stattfinden.
5 **propped up:** aufgestützt, hoch gelegt.
5 f. **to take s.th. in:** etwas wahrnehmen, registrieren.
8 f. **jostling and hooting:** Gedränge und Geschrei.
12 **crank** (coll.): Spinner.
18 **Mojitos** (pl.): Cocktail aus weißem Rum, Limette, Minze, Rohrzucker, Soda und Angostura.
20 **bowtie:** Fliege (Krawatte).

at the El Encanto, I read, garden, burn things in a pan, clean spasmodically, and listen to whatever the local arts station is playing on the radio. When I feel up to it, I work on my novel (working title, *Grandma Rivers*) – either that or my Master's thesis, "Claustrophobia in Franz Kafka's Fictive Universe," now eleven years behind schedule.

I was sitting on the porch late one afternoon – a Monday, my day off, the sun suspended just above the trees, birds slicing the air, every bud and flower entertaining its individual bee – when I heard a woman's voice raised in exasperation from the porch next door. She was trying to reel herself in, fighting to keep her voice from getting away from her, but I couldn't quite make out what she was saying. The woman's voice rose and fell, and then I recognized the voice of my next-door neighbor saying something in reply, something curt and dismissive, punctuated by the end stop of the front door slamming shut.

Next it was the sharp hammer-and-anvil ring of spike heels on pavement – *toing, toing, toing* – as they

2 **spasmodically** (adv.): sporadisch, hin und wieder.
9 **to suspend:** hängen, schweben.
10 **to slice:** (durch)schneiden.
12 **exasperation:** Verzweiflung.
13 **to reel o.s. in** (fig.): sich wieder beruhigen.
18 **curt:** knapp, barsch.
dismissive: abweisend.
19 **punctuated:** unterbrochen, abgebrochen.
21 **hammer-and-anvil ring:** Klang von Hammer und Amboss.
22 **spike heels:** Pfennigabsätze.

retreated down the Schusters' macadam driveway, turned left on the sidewalk, and halted at my gate, which was, of course, locked. I was alert now in every fiber. I slipped a finger between the pages of the novel I'd been reading and held my breath. I heard the gate rattle, my eyes straining to see through the dense leathery mass of the oaks, and then the voice called, "Hello, hello, *hello!*" It was a young voice, female, a take-charge and brook-no-nonsense sort of voice, a very attractive voice, actually, but for some reason I didn't reply. Habit, I suppose. I was on my own porch in my own yard, minding my own business, and I resented the intrusion, no matter what it turned out to be, and I had no illusions on that score either. She was selling something, circulating a petition, organizing a Neighborhood Watch group, looking for a lost cat; she was out of gas, out of money, out of luck. I experienced a brief but vivid recollection of the time the gardener had left the gate ajar and a dark little woman in a sari came rushing up the walk holding a

1 **macadam:** Schotter.
3 **alert:** wachsam, auf der Hut.
6 **to rattle:** klappern.
9f. **brook-no-nonsense sort of voice:** Stimme, die signalisiert: »Ich dulde keinen Unsinn«.
13 **to resent s.th.:** etwas übel nehmen.
intrusion: Störung.
15 **petition:** Unterschriftensammlung.
16 **Neighborhood Watch:** Vereinigung von Bürgern, die in ihrer Nachbarschaft für Sicherheit sorgen.
18 **recollection:** Erinnerung.
19 **ajar:** einen Spaltbreit offen.

balsawood replica of the *Stars & Stripes* out in front of her as if it were made of sugar-frosted air, looked me in the eye, and said, "P'raps maybe you buy for a hunnert dollah good coin monee?"

"I'm your neighbor," the voice called, and the gate rattled again. "Come on," she said, "I can see you, you know – I can see your feet – and I know you're there. I just want to take a minute of your time, that's all, just a minute –"

She could see me? Self-consciously I lifted my feet from the floorboards and propped them up on the rail. "I can't," I said, and my voice sounded weak and watered down, "I'm busy right now."

The fraction of a moment passed, all the sounds of the neighborhood butting up against one another – crows cursing in the trees, a jet revealing itself overhead with the faintest distant whine of its engines, a leaf blower starting up somewhere – and then she sang out, "I like your shoes. Where'd you get them? Not in this town, right?"

I said nothing, but I was listening.

"Come on, just a minute, that's all I ask."

1 **balsawood replica:** Nachbildung aus Balsaholz, Modell.
"Stars & Stripes" (pl.): Name einer Jacht, gewann 1987 den America's Cup für die USA.
3f. **P'raps maybe you buy for a hunnert dollah good coin monee?:** *Perhaps you might like to buy this for a hundred dollars?*
10 **self-consciously** (adv.): unsicher, befangen.
13 **watered down:** verwässert.
14 **fraction:** Bruchteil.
15 **to butt up:** zusammenstoßen, -prallen.
17 **whine:** Heulen.

I may live alone, by preference, but don't get me wrong, I'm no eunuch. I have the same needs and urges as other men, which I've been able to satisfy sporadically with Stefania Porovka, the assistant pastry chef at the hotel. Stefania is thirty-two, with a smoky deep Russian voice that falls somewhere in the range between magnetic and aphrodisiacal and two children in elementary school. The children are all right, as children go, aside from a little caterwauling when they don't get their way (which seems to be about a hundred percent of the time), but I can't manage to picture them in my house, and by the same token, I can't picture myself in Stefania's psychotically disordered two-bedroom walk-up. So what I'm saying is that I got up from the porch and ambled down the walk to the gate and the girl of twenty or so standing there in blue jeans, heels and a V-neck top.

She was leaning over the gate, her arms crossed at the wrists, rings glinting from her fingers. Her eyes and hair were the exact same shade of brown, as if the colors had been mixed in the same vat, which in a sense I guess they were, and she had unusually thick

4f. **pastry chef:** Konditormeister.
7 **aphrodisiacal:** aphrodisisch, den Geschlechtstrieb steigernd.
9 **caterwauling:** Gejaule.
12f. **by the same token:** ebenso.
14 **two-bedroom walk-up** (coll.): Wohnung mit zwei Schlafzimmern in einem Haus ohne Fahrstuhl.
15 **to amble:** schlendern.
19 **to glint:** schimmern, glänzen.
21 **had been mixed in the same vat:** waren wie aus dem gleichen Farbtopf.

and expressive eyegrows of the same color. From where I was standing, five feet back from the locked gate, I could see down the front of her blouse. She wasn't wearing a brassiere. "Hello," I said, regaling her with a cautious nod and the same approximation of a smile I put on for my customers at the bar.

"Oh, *hi*," she returned, giving it the sort of emphasis that said she was surprised and impressed and very, very, friendly. "I'm Samantha. I live up at the end of the block – the big white house with the red trim?"

I nodded. At this point I was noncommittal. She was attractive – pretty and beyond, actually – but too young for me to be interested in anything more than a neighborly way, and as I say, I wasn't especially neighborly to begin with.

"And you are –?"

"Hart," I said, "Hart Simpson," and I put my hands on my hips, wondering if she could translate body language.

She never moved, but for a slight readjustment of her hands that set her bracelets ajingle. She was smiling now, her eyebrows arching up and away from the

4 **brassiere:** Büstenhalter.
4f. **to regale s.o. with s.th.:** jdn. mit etwas bedenken, verwöhnen, erfreuen.
5 **nod:** Kopfnicken.
approximation: (fig.) Annäherung.
10 **trim:** Verzierung(en); Fensterumrandung(en).
11 **noncommittal:** zurückhaltend.
20 **readjustment:** Änderung; hier: veränderte Haltung.
21 **to set s.th. ajingle:** etwas zum Klimpern bringen.
22 **to arch up:** sich wölben.

sudden display of her teeth. “Hart,” she repeated, as if my name were a curious stone she'd found in the street and was busy polishing on the sleeve of her blouse. And then: “Hart, are we bothering you? I mean, are we really bothering you all that much?”

I have to admit the question took me by surprise. Bothering me? I never even knew she existed until thiry seconds ago – and who was this *we* she was referring to? “*We?*” I said.

The smile faded, and she gave me a long, slow look. “So you're not the one who complained – or one of the ones?”

“You must have me confused with somebody else. I don't have the faintest idea what you're talking about.”

“Peep Hall –” she said, “you know, like *peephall.com*?”

It was warm, midsummer, the air charged with the scent of rosemary and lavender and the desiccated menthol of the eucalyptus trees. I felt the sun on my face. I slowly shook my head.

She rubbed the palms of her hands together as if she were washing with soap and water, shifted her eyes away, and then came back to me again. “It's nothing dirty,” she said. “It's not like it's some sleazoid club with a bunch of Taiwanese businessmen shoving

18 **charged:** beladen, erfüllt.
19 **rosemary and lavender:** Rosmarin und Lavendel.
desiccated: getrocknet.
25 **sleazoid** (coll.): schäbig, schmierig (mit anzüglichem Unterton).
26 **to shove:** schieben, stecken.

dollar bills up our crotches or we're lap-dancing or anything like that – we don't even take our clothes off that much, because that totally gets old –"

I still had no idea what she was talking about, but I was beginning to warm to the general drift of it. "Listen," I said, trying to unhinge my smile a bit, "do you want to come in for a beer or maybe a glass of wine or something?"

My house – not the one I grew up in, but this one, the one I inherited from my grandmother – is a shrine to her conventional, turn-of-the-last-century taste, as well as a kind of museum of what my parents left behind when they died. There isn't too much of me in it, but I'm not one for radical change, and the Stickley furniture, the mica lamps, and even the ashtrays and bric-a-brac are wearing well, as eternal as the king's ankus or the treasure buried with Tutankhamen. I keep the place neat – my parents' books commingled

3 **because that totally gets old** (coll.): weil das nicht mehr »in« ist.
5 **general drift:** allgemeine Idee, grobe Vorstellung.
6 **to unhinge:** hier etwa: lösen.
10 **shrine:** Schrein, Heiligtum.
14 **Stickley:** Gustav S. (1858–1942); entwickelte Möbel in einem einfachen, praktischen Stil, bekannt auch als »Craftsman«-Stil.
15 **mica lamp:** Lampen aus Kupfer mit Schirm aus Muskovit; beliebt um die Wende zum 20. Jh., auch im Zusammenhang mit dem »Craftsman«-Stil.
16 **bric-a-brac:** Nippes.
to wear well: gut halten, sehr haltbar sein.
16f. **king's ankus** (fig.): uraltes und sehr wertvolles Objekt (*ankus* [Hindi]: Elefantenstock).
18 **commingled:** vermischt.

with my own on the built-in bookshelves, rugs squared off against the couches and chairs, cups and dishes neatly aligned in the glass-front cabinets – but it's not particularly clean, I'm afraid. I'm not much for dusting. Or vacuuming. The toilets could use a little more attention. And the walls on either side of the fireplace feature long, striated, urine-colored stains where the water got in around the chimney flashing last winter.

"Nice place," Samantha breathed as I handed her a beer and led her into the living room, the house as dark and cool as a wine cellar though it must have been ninety out there in the sun. She settled into the big oak chair by the window, kicked off her heels and took first one foot, then the other, into her hands and slowly rubbed it. "I hate heels," she said, "especially these. But that's what they want us to wear."

I was having a beer too, and I cradled it in my lap and watched her.

"No running shoes – they hate running shoes – and no sweats. It's in our contract." She laughed. "But you don't know what I'm talking about, do you?"

I was thinking about Stefania and how long it had been since I'd had her over, how long it had been

1 f. **squared off:** rechtwinklig angeordnet.
3 **aligned:** in einer Reihe ausgerichtet, aufgestellt.
7 **striated:** streifig.
8 **flashing:** Schutzblech.
13 **ninety:** *ninety degrees Fahrenheit:* 32,2 Grad Celsius.
18 **to cradle:** wiegen, auf dem Schoß halten.
21 **sweats** (pl.): Jogginganzug.
24 **to have s.o. over:** jdn. einladen.

since she'd sat in that chair and done something as unselfconscious as rubbing her bare white feet and laughing over a beer. "Tell me," I said.

It was a long story, involving so many digressions that the digressions became stories in themselves, but finally I began to gather that the big white house on the corner, where she lived with six other girls, was meant to represent a college dorm – that's where the "Peep Hall" designation came in – and that the business of the place was to sell subscriptions on the Internet to overlathered voyeurs who could click on any time of day or night to watch the girls going about their business in living color. "So you've got all these video cameras around," I said, trying to picture it. "Like at the bank or the 7-Eleven – that sort of thing?"

"Yeah, but much better quality, and instead of just like two of them or whatever, you've got cameras all over the place."

"Even in the bathroom?"

Another laugh. "*Especially* the bathroom, what do you think?"

I didn't have anything to say to that. I guess I was shocked. I *was* shocked. I definitely was. But why not

2 **unselfconscious:** unbefangen.
4 **digression:** Abschweifung.
8 **dorm** (coll.): Wohnheim.
9 **designation:** Bezeichnung.
11 **overlathered:** überreizt.
15 **7-Eleven:** amerikanische Supermarktkette; offen von 7 Uhr bis 23 Uhr, sieben Tage die Woche.

admit it? I was titillated too. Women in the shower, I was thinking, women in the tub. I drained my beer, held the bottle up to the light, and asked her if she'd like another one.

She was already slipping her feet back into the shoes. "No, no thanks – I've got to go," she said, rising to her feet. "But thanks for the beer and all – and if they do come around with a petition, you tell them we're not doing anything wrong, okay?" She was smiling, swaying slightly over her heels. "And I don't know if you're into it – you're on-line, right? – but you should check us out, see for yourself."

We were at the door. She handed me the empty beer bottle, still warm from the embrace of her hand. "You really should," she said.

After she left, I opened another beer and wandered through the downstairs rooms, picking up magazines and tossing them back down again, opening and shutting doors for no good reason, until I found myself in the kitchen. There were dishes in the sink, pans encrusted with one thing or another on the stove. The drainboard looked like an artifact, the one incomprehensible object left behind by a vanished civilization, and was it merely decorative or was it

1 **titillated:** angenehm erregt.
10 **to sway:** schwanken, schaukeln, sich hin und her bewegen.
18 **to toss:** werfen.
21 **encrusted:** verkrustet.
22 **drainboard:** Abtropffläche.
22 f. **incomprehensible:** unverständlich.

meant for some utilitarian purpose? The windows were a smudge of light. The plants needed water. I'd been planning to make myself an omelet and then go up to the university for the Monday Night Film Society's showing of *The Seventh Seal*, a film so bleak it always brought tears of hysterical laughter to my eyes, but instead, on an impulse, I dialed Stefania's number. When she answered, there was an edge to her voice, all the Russian smoke blown right out of it by the winds of complexity and turmoil, and in the background I could hear the children shrieking as if the skin were being peeled from their bodies in long, tapering strips. "Hello?" Stefania demanded. "Who is it? Is anybody there? Hello?" Very carefully, though my hand was trembling, I replaced the receiver in its cradle.

And this was strange: it was my day off, the only day of the week when I could really relax, and yet I was all worked up, as if I'd had one too many cups of coffee. I found myself drifting through the house again, thoughtfully pulling at my beer, studying a

2 **smudge of light:** verschmierte Fläche, durch die das Licht fällt.
5 **"The Seventh Seal":** Film von Ingmar Bergman (1957) über die Zeit der Pest im Europa des 14. Jh.s (*seal:* Siegel).
bleak: öde, trostlos.
8f. **there was an edge to her voice:** es war eine Spur Nervosität, Gereiztheit in ihrer Stimme.
10 **turmoil:** Aufruhr, Durcheinander.
11 **to shriek:** gellend schreien.
13 **tapering:** spitz zulaufend.
16 **cradle:** (Telefon-)Gabel.
21 **to pull:** nippen.

lamp or a painting or an old family photo as if I'd never seen it before, all the while making a wide circuit around the little room off the front hall where the computer sat on my desk like a graven idol. I resisted it for half an hour or more, until I realized I was resisting it, and then I sat down, booted it up and clicked on *www.peephall.com.*

A Web page gradually took shape on the screen. I saw the house on the corner, a big shapeless stucco box against a neutral background, and in front of it, as the image filled in from top to bottom, the girls began to materialize. There were seven of them, squeezed shoulder-to-shoulder to fit in the frame, and they were dressed in low-cut tops and smiling as if they were selling lip gloss or plaque remover. Samantha was second from the left, staring right at me. "*Twenty-four hours a day!*" screamed the teaser. "*Watch our young sexy College Girls take bubble baths, throw sexy Lingerie parties and sunbathe Nude poolside! You'll never miss an Intimate Moment!*" To the left, in a neat pulsating sidebar, were come-ons for related sites, like *See Me Pee* and *Hot Sexy Teen*

4 **graven idol:** Götzenbild.
9 **stucco:** Stuck; Stuckatur.
15 **plaque remover:** Zahnbelagentferner.
17 **teaser:** Aufmacher (Werbung).
19 **lingerie:** Unterwäsche.
nude: nackt.
21 **to pulsate:** pulsieren.
sidebar: Spalte.
come-on (coll.): Anmacher.
22 **to pee:** pinkeln.

Vixens. The subscription fee was $36 a month. I never hesitated.

Once I was in, I was presented with an array of choices. There were forty cameras in all, and I could choose among the two bathrooms, three bedrooms, the pool, kitchen, living room and deck. I was working on my third beer – on an empty stomach, no less – and I wasn't really thinking, just moving instinctively toward something I couldn't have defined. My pulse was racing. I felt guilty, paranoiac, consumed with sadness and lust. The phrase *dirty old man* shot through my head, and I clicked on "The Kitchen" because I couldn't go to "Upstairs Bath," not yet anyway.

The room that came into view was neat, preternaturally neat, like the set for a cooking show, saucepans suspended from hooks, ceramic containers of flour, sugar, tea and coffee lined up along a tile counter, matching dishtowels hanging from two silver loops affixed to the cabinet beneath the sink. But of course it *was* a set, the whole house was a set, because that was what this was all about: seeing through walls like Superman, like God. I clicked on Camera 2,

1 **vixen:** Luder.
3 **array:** Aufstellung, Ansammlung.
6 **deck:** Sonnenterrasse.
10 **paranoiac:** paranoid.
(to be) **consumed with s.th.:** sich vor etwas verzehren.
14 f. **preternaturally neat:** außergewöhnlich aufgeräumt und sauber.
17 f. **tile counter:** gekachelte Arbeitsfläche.
18 **dishtowel:** Geschirrtuch.
19 **loop:** Schlaufe, Haken.
affixed: befestigt.

and suddenly a pair of shoulders appeared on the screen, female shoulders, clad in gray and with a blond ponytail centered in the frame. The shoulders ducked out of view, came back again, working vigorously, furiously, over something, and now the back of a blond head was visible, a young face in profile, and I experienced my first little *frisson* of discovery: she was beating eggs in a bowl. The sexy young teen college vixens were having omelets for dinner, just like me … but no, another girl was there now, short hair, almost boyish, definitely not Samantha, and she had a cardboard box in her hand, and they were – what were they doing? – they were making brownies. *Brownies.* I could have cried for the simple sweet irreducible beauty of it.

That night – and it was a long night, a night that stretched on past the declining hours and into the building ones – I never got out of the kitchen. Samantha appeared at twenty past six, just as the blonde (Traci) pulled the brownies from the oven, and in the next five minutes the entire cast appeared, fourteen hands hovering over the hot pan, fingers to mouths, fat dark crumbs on their lips, on the front of their T-shirts and clingy tops, on the unblemished tiles of

2 **clad:** gekleidet.
7 **frisson:** Schauer.
13 **brownies** (pl.): kleiner Schokoladenkuchen.
14 f. **irreducible:** nicht reduzierbar.
17 **declining hours** (pl.): früher Morgen.
22 **to hover:** schweben.
24 **clingy:** eng anliegend.
unblemished: makellos.

the counter and floor. They poured milk, juice, iced tea, Coke, and they flowed in and out of chairs, propped themselves up against the counter, the refrigerator, the dishwasher, every movement and gesture a revelation. And more: they chattered, giggled, made speeches, talked right through one another, their faces animated with the power and fluency of their silent words. What were they saying? What were they thinking? Already I was spinning off the dialogue ("Come on, don't be such a pig, leave some for somebody else!"; "Yeah, and who you think went and dragged her ass down to the store to pick up the mix in the first place?"), and it was like no novel, no film, no experience I'd ever had. Understand me: I'd seen girls together before, seen them talk, overheard them, and men and women and children too, but this was different. This was for me. My private performance. And Samantha, the girl who'd come up my walk in a pair of too-tight heels, was the star of it.

The next morning I was up at first light, and I went straight to the computer. I needed to shave, comb my hair, dress, eat, micturate; I needed to work on my novel, jog up and down the steps at the university stadium, pay bills, read the paper, take the car in for an

3 **to prop o.s. up:** sich gegen etwas lehnen.
5 **to chatter:** schwatzen.
to giggle: kichern.
9 **to spin s.th. off:** etwas abspulen.
12 **to drag one's ass somewhere** (vulg.): den Arsch irgendwo hinbewegen.
15 **to overhear s.o.:** jdn. belauschen.
22 **to micturate:** urinieren.

oil change. The globe was spinning. People were up, alert, ready for the day. But I was sitting in a cold dark house, wrapped in a blanket, checking in on Peep Hall.

Nobody was stirring. I'd watched Samantha and the short-haired girl (Gina) clean up the kitchen the night before, sweeping up the crumbs, stacking plates and glasses in the dishwasher, setting the brownie pan out on the counter to soak, and then I'd watched the two of them sit at the kitchen table with their books and a boombox, turning pages, taking notes, rocking to the beat of the unheard music. Now I saw the pan sitting on the counter, a peach-colored band of sunlight on the wall behind it, plates stacked in the drainboard, the silver gleam of the microwave – and the colors weren't really true, I was thinking, not true at all. I studied the empty kitchen in a kind of trance, and then, without ceremony, I clicked on "Upstairs Bath." There were two cameras, a shower cam and a toilet cam, and both gazed bleakly out on nothing. I went to "Downstairs Bath" then, and was rewarded by a blur of motion as the stone-faced figure of one of the girls – it was Cyndi, or no, Candi – slouched into the room a flannel nightdress, hiked it up in back, and sat

6 **to stack:** einräumen, stapeln.
8 **to soak:** einweichen.
10 **boombox** (coll.): Radiogerät mit starken, dröhnenden Lautsprechern.
19 **bleakly** (adv.): niedergeschlagen.
20 **blur:** verschwommener Fleck.
22 **to slouch:** latschen.
23 **flannel:** Flanell.
to hike s.th. up: etwas anheben, hochziehen.

heavily on the toilet. Her eyes were closed – she was still dreaming. There was the sleepy slow operation with the toilet paper, a perfunctory rinsing of the fingertips, and then she was gone. I clicked on the bedrooms then, all three of them in succession, until I found Samantha, a gently respiring presence beneath a quilt in a single bed against the far wall. She was curled away from me, her hair spilled out over the pillow. I don't know what I was feeling as I watched her there, asleep and oblivious, every creep, sadist, pervert and masturbator with thirty-six dollars in his pocket leering at her, but it wasn't even remotely sexual. It went far beyond that, far beyond. I just watched her, like some sort of tutelary spirit, watched her till she turned over and I could see the dreams invade her eyelids.

I was late for work that day – I work lunch on Tuesdays and Thursdays, then come back in at five for my regular shift – but it was slow and nobody seemed to notice. A word on the hotel: it's a pretty little place on the European model, perched at the top of the tallest hill around, and it has small but elegant rooms, and a cultivated – or at least educated – staff. It fea-

3 **perfunctory:** flüchtig.
6 **to respire:** atmen.
7 **quilt:** Bettdecke.
10 **oblivious:** weltvergessen.
creep (coll.): Fiesling.
12 **to leer:** lüstern blicken.
14 **tutelary spirit:** Schutzgeist.
21 **to be perched:** thronen.

tures a restaurant with pretensions to three-star status, a cozy bar and a patio with a ten-million-dollar view of the city and the harbor spread out beneath it. The real drinkers – university wives, rich widows, department heads entertaining visiting lecturers – don't come in for lunch till one o'clock or later, so in my absence the cocktail waitress was able to cover for me, pouring two glasses of sauvignon blanc and uncapping a bottle of non-alcoholic beer all on her own. Not that I didn't apologize profusely – I might have been eleven years late with my thesis, but work I took seriously.

It was a typical day on the South Coast, seventy-two at the beach, eighty or so on the restaurant patio, and we did get busy for a while there. I found myself shaking martinis and Manhattans, uncorking bottles of merlot and viognier, cutting up whole baskets of fruit for the sweet rum drinks that seemed to be in vogue again. It was work – simple, repetitive non-intellectual – and I lost myself in it. When I looked up again, it was ten of three and the lunch crowd was dispersing. Suddenly I felt exhausted, as if I'd been out on some careening debauch the night before instead

1 **pretensions:** Ambitionen.
2 **patio:** Veranda, Terrasse.
7 **to cover for s.o.:** jdn. vertreten, für jdn. einspringen.
10 **profusely** (adv.): vielmals, überschwänglich.
16 **Manhattan:** Cocktail aus Whisky, Wermut und Angostura.
18 f. **in vogue:** en vogue, in Mode.
19 **repetitive:** monoton.
21 f. **to disperse:** sich auflösen, zerstreuen.
23 **careening debauch:** Orgie.

of sitting in front of my computer till my eyes began to sag. I punched out, drove home and fell into bed as if I'd been hit in the back of the head with a board.

I'd set the alarm for four-thirty, to give myself time to run the electric razor over my face, change my shirt and get back to work, and that would have been fine, but for the computer. I checked the walnut clock on the mantel as I was knotting my tie – I had ten minutes to spare – and sat down at my desk to have a quick look at Peep Hall. For some reason – variety's sake, I guess – I clicked on "Living Room Cam 1," and saw that two of the girls, Mandy and Traci, were exercising to a programm on TV. In the nude. They were doing jumping jacks when the image first appeared on the screen, hands clapping over their heads, breasts flouncing, and then they switched, in perfect unison, to squat thrusts, their faces staring into the camera, their arms flexed, legs kicking out behind. It was a riveting performance. I watched, in awe, as they went on to aerobics, some light lifting with three-pound dumbbells and what looked to be a

2 **to sag:** zufallen (Augen).
I punched out: ich stempelte meine Stechkarte.
8 **mantel:** Kaminsims.
13 **in the nude:** nackt.
14 **jumping jack:** Hampelmann (Turnübung).
16 **to flounce:** (sich) stolz präsentieren, zur Schau stellen.
17 **unison:** Übereinstimmung.
squat thrust: Stützstrecke (Turnübung).
18 **flexed:** gebeugt.
19 **riveting:** fesselnd, faszinierend.
19 f. **in awe:** ehrfurchtsvoll.
21 **dumbbell:** Hantel.

lead-weighted cane, and finally concluded by toweling each other off. I was twenty minutes late for work.

This time it wasn't all right. Jason, the manager, was behind the bar when I came in, and the look on his face told me he wasn't especially thrilled at having this unlooked-for opportunity to dole out cocktail onions and bar mix to a roomful of sunburned hotel guests, enchanted tourists and golfers warming up for dinner. He didn't say a word. Just dropped what he was doing (frothing a mango margarita in the blender), brushed past me and hurried down the corridor to his office as if the work of the world awaited him there. He was six years younger than I, he had a Ph. D. in history from a university far more prestigious than the one that ruled our little burg, and he wielded a first-rate vocabulary. I could have lived without him. At any rate, I went around to each customer with a smile on my face – even the lunatic in

1 **cane:** Spazierstock.
1 f. **to towel each other off:** sich gegenseitig trocken reiben.
6 **to dole out** (coll.): aus-, verteilen.
8 **enchanted:** entzückt.
to warm up (coll.): in Schwung kommen, sich in Stimmung bringen.
10 **to froth:** aufschäumen.
mango margarita: Cocktail aus Limone, Limonensaft, Eiswürfel, Tequila und Mangolikör.
11 **blender:** Mixer.
14 f. **prestigious:** angesehen, mit Prestige.
15 **burg** (coll.): Stadt.
16 **to wield a first-rate vocabulary:** einen erstklassigen Wortschatz haben.
18 **lunatic:** Irre(r).

tam-o'-shanter and plus fours drinking rum and Red Bull at the far end of the bar – and refreshed drinks, bar napkins and the bowls of pretzels and bar mix. I poured with a heavy hand.

Around seven, the dining room began to fill up. This was my favorite hour of the day, the air fragrant and still, the sun picking out individual palms and banks of flowers to illuminate as it sank into the ocean, people bending to their hors d'oeuvres with a kind of quiet reverence, as if for once they really were thankful for the bounty spread out before them. Muted snatches of conversation drifted in from the patio. Canned piano music – something very familiar – seeped out of the speakers. All was well, and I poured myself a little Irish whiskey to take some of the tightness out of my neck and shoulders.

That was when Samantha walked in.

She was with two other girls – Gina, I recognized; the other one, tall, athletic, with a nervous, rapid-blinking gaze that seemed to reduce the whole place

1 **tam-o'-shanter:** schottische Baskenmütze.
plus fours (pl.): Knickerbocker.
3 **napkin:** Serviette.
4 **I poured with a heavy hand:** ich schenkte großzügig ein.
6 **fragrant:** duftend.
9 **hors d'oeuvres:** Vorspeise(n).
10 **reverence:** Ehrfurcht.
11 **bounty:** reiche Fülle.
12 **muted:** gedämpft.
snatches of conversation: Gesprächsfetzen.
13 **canned music:** Musikberieselung ‚aus der Konserve'.
14 **to seep:** sickern, dringen.
20 **gaze:** Blick.

and everything in it to a series of snapshots, was unfamiliar. All three were wearing sleek ankle-length dresses that left their shoulders bare, and as they leaned into the hostess' stand there was the glint of jewelry at their ears and throats. My mouth went dry. I felt as if I'd been caught out at something desperate, something furtive and humiliating, though they were all the way across the room and Samantha hadn't even so much as glanced in my direction. I fidgeted with the wine key and tried not to stare, and then Frankie, the hostess, was leading them to a table out on the patio.

I realized I was breathing hard, and my pulse must have shot up like a rocket, and for what? She probably wouldn't even recognize me. We'd shared a beer for twenty minutes. I was old enough to be her – her what? Her uncle. I needed to get a grip. She wasn't the one watching *me* through a hidden lens. "Hart? Hart, are you there?" a voice was saying, and I looked up to see Megan, the cocktail waitress, hovering over her station with a drink order on her lips.

"Yeah, sure," I said, and I took the order and started in on the drinks. "By the way," I said as casu-

2 **sleek:** elegant.
4 **glint:** Funkeln.
7 **furtive:** heimlich.
humiliating: demütigend, beschämend.
9 **to fidget:** herumfummeln.
10 **wine key:** Korkenzieher.
21 **to hover:** wartend herumstehen.

ally as I could, "you know that table of three – the girls who just came in? Tell me when you take their order, okay? Their drinks are on me."

As it turned out, they weren't having any of the sweet rum drinks garnished with fruit and a single orange nasturtium flower or one of our half dozen margaritas or even the house chardonnay by the glass. "I carded them," Megan said, "and they're all legal, but what they want is three sloe gin fizzes. Do we even have sloe gin?"

In the eight years I'd been at the El Encanto, I doubt if I'd mixed more than three or four sloe gin fizzes, and those were for people whose recollections of the Eisenhower administration were still vivid. But we did have a vestigial bottle of sloe gin in the back room, wedged between the peppermint schnapps and the Benedictine, and I made them their drinks. Frankie had seated them around the corner on the patio, so I couldn't see how the fizzes went over, and then a series of orders came leapfrogging in, and I started pouring and mixing and forgot all about it. The next time I looked up, Samantha was coming across the

5 **garnished:** verziert, garniert.
6 **nasturtium:** Kapuzinerkresse.
8 **to card s.o.** (coll.): den Ausweis von jdm. verlangen.
they're all legal (coll.): sie sind alle volljährig.
9 **sloe gin:** Schlehenschnaps.
14 **Eisenhower administration:** Dwight D. Eisenhower (1890–1969) war 1953–61 Präsident der USA.
15 **vestigial bottle:** übrig gebliebene Flasche.
16 **wedged:** eingezwängt.
20 **to leapfrog:** nach und nach eintreffen.

room to me, her eyebrows dancing over an incipient smile. I could see she was having trouble with her heels and the constriction of the dress – or gown, I suppose you'd call it – and I couldn't help thinking how young she looked, almost like a little girl playing dress-up. "Hart," she said, resting her hands on the bar so that I could admire her sculpted fingers and her collection of rings – rings even on her thumps – "I didn't know you worked here. This place is really nice."

"Yeah," I said, grinning back at her while holding the picture of her in my head, asleep, with her hair splayed out over the pillow. "It's first-rate. Top-notch. Really fantastic. It's a great place to work."

"You know, that was relly sweet of you," she said.

I wanted to say something like "Aw, shucks" or "No problem," but instead I heard myself say, "The gesture or the drink?"

She looked at me quizzically a moment, and then let out a single soft flutter of a laugh. "Oh, you mean the gin fizzes?" And she laughed again – or giggled, actually. "I'm legal today, did you know that? And my gramma made me promise to have a sloe gin fizz so

1 f. **incipient smile:** Anflug von Lächeln (*incipient:* aufkommend, beginnend).
3 **constriction:** Behinderung, Einengung.
7 **sculpted:** wie gemeißelt, wohlgeformt.
13 **splayed out:** ausgebreitet.
top-notch (coll.): klasse, eins a.
16 **shucks** (coll.): Quatsch!
19 **quizzically** (adv.): fragend.
20 **flutter of a laugh:** kurzes Lachen.

she could be here tonight in spirit – she passed last winter? – but I think we're having like a bottle of white wine or something with dinner. That's my sister I'm with – she's taking me out for my birthday, along with Gina – she's one of my roommates? But you probably already know that, right?"

I shot my eyes left, then right, up and down the bar. All the drinks were fresh, and no one was paying us the least attention. "What do you mean?"

Her eyebrows lifted, the silky thick eyebrows that were like two strips of mink pasted to her forehead, and her hair was like some exotic fur too, rich and shining and dark. "You didn't check out the Web site?"

"No," I lied.

"Well, you ought to," she said. The air was a stew of smells – a couple at the end of the bar were sharing the warm spinach and scallop salad, there was the sweet burnt odor of the Irish whiskey I was sipping from a mug, Samantha's perfume (or was it Megan's?) and a medley of mesquite-grilled chops and braised fish and Peter Oxendine's famous sauces wafting in from the kitchen. "Okay," she said, shaking out her

1 **to pass:** versterben.
11 **mink:** Nerz.
16f. **stew of smells:** Mischung verschiedener Gerüche.
18 **scallop:** Muschel.
19 **odor:** Geruch.
21 **medley:** Gemisch.
mesquite-grilled: über Holzkohle gegrillt.
braised: geschmort.
22 **to waft:** wehen.

hair with a flick of her head and running a quick look around the place before bringing her eyes back to me. "Okay, well – I just wanted to say thanks." She shrugged. "I guess I better be getting back to the girls."

"Yeah," I said. "Nice seeing you again. And hey, happy birthday."

She'd already turned away from the bar, earrings swaying, face composed, but she stopped to give me a smile over her shoulder, and then she made her way across the room and out onto the darkened patio.

And that would have been it, at least until I could get home and watch her shimmy out of that gown and paint her toenails or gorge on cake or whatever it was she was going to do in the semi-privacy of her own room, but I couldn't let it go and I sent over dessert too, a truly superior raspberry-kiwi tart Stefania had whipped up that afternoon. That really put them in my debt, and after dessert the three of them came to the bar to beam at me and settle in for coffee and an after-dinner drink. "You're really just twenty-one today?" I said, grinning at Samantha till the roots of my teeth must have showed. "You're sure I don't have to card you, now, right?"

1 **flick:** kurze Bewegung.
4 **to shrug:** die Achseln zucken.
9 **composed:** gefasst, ruhig.
13 **to shimmy out:** herausschlüpfen.
14 **to gorge on s.th.:** etwas verschlingen.
18 **to whip s.th. up** (coll.): etwas schnell (zu essen) machen.
20 **to beam:** übers ganze Gesicht strahlen.

I watched the hair swirl round her shoulders as she braced herself against the bar and reached down to ease off her heels, and then she was fishing through her purse till she came up with her driver's license and laid it out proudly on the bar. I picked it up and held it to the light – there she was, grinning wide out of the bottom right-hand corner, date of birth clearly delineated, and her name, Jennifer B. Knickish, spelled out in bold block letters. "Jennifer?" I said.

She took the card back a frown, her eyebrows closing ranks. "Everybody calls me Samantha," she said. "Really." And to her companions: "Right, guys?" I watched them nod their glossy heads. The older one, the sister, giggled. "And besides, I don't want any of the creeps to know my real name – even my first name – you know what I mean?"

Oh, yes, yes I did. And I smiled and bantered and called up reserves of charm I hadn't used in years, and the drinks were on me all night long. It was Samantha's birthday, wasn't it? And her twenty-first, no less – a rite of passage if ever there was one. I poured Grand Marnier and Rémy till the customers disappeared and the waiters and busboys slipped out the back and the lights drew down to nothing.

1 **to swirl:** wirbeln.
2 **to brace o.s.:** sich (ab)stützen.
8 **to delineate:** sich (deutlich) abzeichnen.
10 **frown:** Stirnrunzeln.
10f. **to close ranks:** sich zusammenschließen, eine Linie bilden.
17 **to banter:** necken.
21 **rite of passage:** Übergangsritual.
23 **busboy:** Bedienungshilfe.

I woke with a headache. I'd matched them, round for round, and, as I say, I'd started in on the Irish whiskey earlier in the night – and yes, I'm all too well aware that the concrete liver and stumbling tongue are hazards of the profession, but I'm pretty good at keeping all that in check. I do get bored, though, and wind up over-doing it from time to time, especially when the novel isn't going well, and it hadn't been going well in a long while. The problem was, I couldn't get past the initial idea – the setup – which was a story I'd come across in the newspaper two or three years ago. It had to do with an old woman's encounter with the mysterious forces of nature (I don't recall her real name, not that it would matter, but I called her Grandma Rivers, to underscore the irony that here was a woman with eight children, thirty-two grandchildren and six great-grandchildren and she was living alone in a trailer park in a part of the country so bleak no one who wasn't condemned to it would ever even deign to glance down on it from the silvered window of a jetliner at thirty-five thousand feet). One night, when the wind was sweeping up out of the south with

4 **concrete liver:** Leber aus Beton.
stumbling: stockend.
5f. **to keep s.th. in check:** etwas in Schach halten.
6f. **to wind up doing s.th.** (coll.): damit, dabei enden, etwas zu tun.
13 **to recall s.th.:** sich an etwas erinnern.
15 **to underscore s.th.:** etwas unterstreichen.
18 **trailer park:** Wohnwagenpark.
19 **to be condemned to s.th.:** zu etwas verurteilt sein.
20 **to deign to do s.th.:** sich herablassen, etwas zu tun.
to glance: einen Blick werfen.

the smell of paradise on it and all her neighbors were mewed up in their aluminium boxes lulled by booze, prescription drugs and the somnolent drone of the tube, she stepped outside to take in the scent of the night and indulge in a cigarette (she always smoked outside so as not to pollute the interior of her own little aluminium box set there on the edge of the scoured prairie). No sooner had she lit up than a fox – a red fox, *Vulpes fulva* – shot out of the shadows and latched onto her ankle. In the shock and confusion of that moment, she lurched back, lost her balance and fell heavily on her right side, dislocating her hip. But the fox, which later proved to be rabid, came right back at her, at her face this time, and the only thing she could think to do in her panic was to seize hold of it with her trembling old arms and pin it beneath her to keep the snapping jaws away from her.

Twelve hours. That's how long she lay there, unable to move, the fox snarling and writhing beneath her, its heartbeat joined to hers, its breathing, the eloquent

2 **mewed up:** eingesperrt.
lulled: eingelullt.
booze (coll.): Alkohol.
3f. **somnolent drone of the tube:** einschläferndes Summen, Brummen des Fernsehers.
8 **scoured:** ausgewaschen (Erdboden), leer gefegt.
10 **to latch onto s.th.** (coll.): sich an etwas festbeißen, in etwas verbeißen.
11 **to lurch back:** zurücktaumeln.
12 **to dislocate s.th.:** (sich) etwas ver-, ausrenken.
13 **rabid:** tollwütig.
19 **to snarl:** knurren.
to writhe: sich krümmen, sich winden.
20 **eloquent:** gewandt; beredt.

movement of its fluids and juices and the workings of its demented little vulpine brain, until somebody – a neighbor – happened to glance beyond the hedge and the hump of the blistered old Jeep Wagoneer her late husband had left behind to see her there, stretched out in the gravel drive like a strip of discarded carpet. Yes. But what then? That was what had me stumped. I thought of going back and tracing her life up to that point, her girlhood in the Depression, her husband's overseas adventures in the war, the son killed in Vietnam … or maybe just to let her sink into the background while I focused on the story of the community, the benighted neighbors and their rat-faced children, so that the trailer park itself became a character. …

But, as I say, I woke with a headache, and when I did sit down at the computer, it wasn't to call up Grandma Rivers and the imperfect dream of her life, but to click onto *peephall.com* and watch another sort of novel unfold before my eyes, one in which the plot

1 **fluids and juices:** Körpersäfte.
2 **demented:** verrückt.
vulpine: schlau, listig.
4 **hump:** hier: Dach.
blistered: ausgebeult.
Jeep Wagoneer: 1962 eingeführtes Fahrzeug, das den Prototyp für alle modernen Mehrzweckfahrzeuge bildete.
6 **gravel:** Kies.
discarded: weggeworfen, ausrangiert.
7 **what had me stumped** (coll.): was mich durcheinander gebracht, ratlos gemacht hatte.
9 **Depression:** Wirtschaftskrise in den USA der 1930er-Jahre.
13 **benighted:** unbedarft.

was out of control and the details were selected and shaped only by the anonymous subscriber with his anonymous mouse. I went straight to Samantha's bedroom, but her bed was empty save for the jumbled topography of pillows and bedclothes, and I stared numbly at the shadows thickening round the walls, at the limp form of the gown tossed over a chair, and checked my watch. It was ten-thirty. *Breakfast*, I thought. I clicked on "Kitchen," but that wasn't her staring into the newspaper with a cup of coffee clenched in one hand and a Power Bar in the other, nor was that her bent at the waist and peering into the refrigerator as if for enlightenment. I went to the living room, but it was empty, a dully flickering static space caught in the baleful gaze of my screen. Had she gone out already? To an early class maybe?

But then I remembered she was taking only one class – "Intermediate Sketching," paid for by the Web site operators, who were encouraging the Sexy Teen College Coeds actually to enroll so that all the voyeurs out there could live the fantasy of seeing

4f. **jumbled topography:** etwa: zerwühlte Oberfläche.
6 **numbly** (adv.): gefühllos, wie betäubt.
7 **limp:** schlaff.
11 **to clench:** umklammert halten.
12 **to peer:** spähen, lugen.
13 **enlightenment:** Aufklärung, Erleuchtung.
14 **flickering:** flimmernd.
15 **baleful:** unheilvoll, traurig.
18 **intermediate:** Mittelstufen-.
20 **coed:** Studentin.
to enroll: sich anmelden, einschreiben.

them hitting the books in their thong bikinis and lacy push-up bras – and that the class met in the afternoon. She was getting paid too, incidentally – five hundred dollars a month, plus the rent-free accommodations at Peep Hall and a food allowance – and all for allowing the world to watch her live hot sexy young life through each scintillating minute of the over-inflated day, the orotund month and the full, round year. I thought of the girls who posed naked for the art classes back when I was an undergraduate (specifically, I thought of Nancy Beckers, short, black hair, balls of muscle in her calves and upper arms and a look in her eyes that made me want to strip to my socks and join her on the dais), and then I clicked on "Downstairs Bath," and there she was.

This wasn't a hot sexy moment. Anything but. Samantha – my Samantha – was crouched over the toilet on her knees, the soles of her feet like single quotes around the swell of her buttocks, her hair spilling over the bright rim of the porcelain bowl. I couldn't see her face, but I watched the back of her

1 **thong bikini:** Tangaslip-Bikini.
lacy: spitzenbesetzt.
2 **bra:** Kurzform von *brassiere.*
7 **scintillating:** faszinierend.
8 **over-inflated:** prall gefüllt.
orotund: volltönend.
14 **dais:** Podium.
17 **to be crouched:** kauern.
18f. **single quotes:** einfache Anführungszeichen.
19 **swell:** Rundung.
buttocks (pl.): Hintern.
20 **rim:** Rand.

head jerk forward as each spasm racked her, and I couldn't help playing the sound track in my mind, feeling sorrowful and guilty at the same time. Her feet – I felt sorry for her feet – and the long sudden shiver of her spine and even the dangling wet ends of her hair. I couldn't watch this. I couldn't. My finger was on the mouse – I took one more look, watched one last shudder ascend her spine and fan out across her shoulder blades, watched her head snap forward and her hair slide loose, and then I clicked off and left her to suffer in private.

A week rolled by, and I hardly noticed. I wasn't sleeping well, wasn't exercising, wasn't sitting on the porch with a book in my hand and the world opening up around me like a bigger book. I was living the life of the screen, my bones gone hollow, my brain dead. I ate at my desk, microwave pizza and chili-cheese burritos, nachos, whiskey in a glass like a slow, sweet promise that was never fulfilled. My scalp itched. My eyes ached. But I don't think I spent a waking moment outside work when I wasn't stalking the rooms

1 **spasm:** Krampf.
to rack: schütteln.
5 **shiver:** Beben, Erzittern.
spine: Rückgrat.
to dangle: herabhängen.
8 **to ascend:** aufsteigen.
17f. **burrito** (Mex. Span.): gerollte Tortilla mit Füllung.
18 **nacho** (Mex. Span.): belegte Tortilla.
19 **scalp:** Kopfhaut.
21 **to stalk s.th.:** sich an etwas heranpirschen; um etwas herumschleichen.

of Peep Hall, clicking from camera to camera in search of a new angle, a better one, the view that would reveal all. I watched Gina floss her teeth and Candi pluck fine translucent hairs from the mole at the corner of her mouth, sat there in the upstairs bath with Traci as she bleached her roots and shaved her legs, hung electrified over the deck as Cyndi perched naked on the railing with a bottle of vodka and a cigarette lighter, breathing fire into the gloom of the gathering night. Mainly, though, I watched Samantha. When she was home, I followed her from room to room, and when she picked up her purse and went out the door, I felt as if Peep Hall had lost its focus. It hurt me, and it was almost like a physical hurt, as if I'd been dealt an invisible blow.

I was pulling into the drive one afternoon – it must have been a Monday or Wednesday, because I'd just worked lunch – when a rangy, tall woman in a pair of wraparound sunglasses came out of nowhere to block my way. She was wearing running shorts and a T-shirt that advertised some fund-raising event at the local elementary school, and she seemed to be out of breath or out of patience, as if she'd been chasing

3 **to floss one's teeth:** sich die Zähne mit Zahnseide reinigen.
4 **translucent:** lichtdurchlässig.
mole: Leberfleck.
6 **to bleach:** bleichen, blondieren.
9 **gloom:** Dunkel.
18 **rangy:** langgliedrig.
19 **wraparound sunglasses** (pl.): Sonnenbrille mit leicht gebogenen Gläsern und Bügeln, die sich an die Gesichtsform anpassen.
21 **fund-raising event:** Benefizveranstaltung.

after me for miles. I was trying to place her as the gate slowly cranked open on its long balky chain to reveal the green depths of the yard beyond – she was someone I knew, or was expected to know. But before I could resolve the issue, she'd looped around the hood of the car and thrust her face in the open window, so close to me now I could see the fine hairs catching the light along the parabola of her jawbone and her shadowy eyes leaping at the lenses of her sunglasses. "I need you to sign this," she said, shoving a clipboard at me.

The gate hit the end of the chain with a clank that made the posts shudder. I just stared at her. "It's me," she said, removing the sunglasses to reveal two angry red welts on the bridge of her nose and a pair of impatient eyes, "Sarah. Sarah Schuster – your nextdoor neighbor?"

I could smell the fumes of the car as it rumbled beneath me, quietly misfiring. "Oh, yeah," I said, "sure," and I attempted a smile.

"You need to sign this," she repeated.

"What is it?"

2 **to crank s.th. open:** etwas mühsam öffnen.
balky: widerspenstig.
5 **to loop around s.th.:** um etwas herumgehen.
6 **to thrust:** schieben, stecken.
8 **parabola:** Parabel, Kurve, Wölbung.
11 **clipboard:** Klemmbrett.
15 **welt:** Striemen.
bridge of the nose: Nasenbein, Sattel.
18 **to rumble:** rumpeln.
19 **to misfire:** Fehlzündungen haben.

"A petition. To get rid of them. Because this is a residential neighborhood – this is a *family* neighborhood – and frankly Steve and I are outraged, just outraged, I mean, as if there isn't enough of this sort of thing going on in town already –"

"Get rid of who?" I said, but I already knew.

I watched her face as she filled me in, the rolling eyes, the clamp and release of the long mortal jaws, moral outrage underscored by a heavy dose of irony, because she was an educated woman, after all, a liberal and a Democrat, but this was just – well, it was just too much.

I didn't need this. I didn't want it. I wanted to be in my own house minding my own business. "All right, yeah," I said, pushing the clipboard back at her, "but I'm real busy right now – can you come back later?"

And then I was rolling up the driveway, the gate already rumbling shut behind me. I was agitated and annoyed – *Sarah Schuster*, who did she think she was? – and the first thing I did when I got in the house was pull the shades and turn on the computer. I checked Peep Hall to be sure Samantha was there – and she was, sunk into the couch in T-shirt and jeans, watching TV with Gina – and then I smoothed back my hair in the mirror and went out the front door. I

2 **residential neighborhood:** (reine) Wohngegend.
3 **outraged:** empört.
7 **to fill s.o. in** (coll.): jdm. alles erzählen, jdn. aufklären.
8 **clamp and release:** ruckartiges Zuschnappen und Öffnen.
21 **to pull the shades:** die Rollläden, Jalousien herunterlassen.
24 **to smooth:** zurückstreichen, glätten.

looked both ways before swinging open the gate, wary of Sarah Schuster and her ilk, but aside from two kids on bikes at the far end of the block, the street was deserted.

Still, I started off in the opposite direction from the big white house on the corner, then crossed the street and kept going – all the way up the next block over – so as to avoid any prying eyes. The sun was warm on my face, my arms were swinging, my feet knew just what to do – I was walking, actually walking through the neighborhood, and it felt good. I noticed things the view from the car window wouldn't have revealed, little details, a tree in fruit here, a new flowerbed there, begonias blooming at the base of three pale silvery eucalypti at the side of a neighbor's house, and all that would have been fine but for the fact that my heart seemed to be exploding in my chest. I saw myself ringing the doorbell, mounting the steps of the big white house and ringing the bell, but beyond that I couldn't quite picture the scene. Would Samantha – or Traci or Candi or whoever – see me as just another one of the creeps she had to chat with on-line for two hours each week as part of her job description? Would she shut the door in my face? Invite *me* in for a beer?

As it turned out, Cyndi answered the door. She was shorter than I'd imagined, and she was dressed in a red halter top and matching shorts, her feet bare and

2 **to be wary of s.o.:** sich vor jdm. in Acht nehmen.
her ilk: ihresgleichen.
8 **prying eyes:** neugierige Blicke.

toenails painted blue – or aquamarine, I suppose you'd call it. I couldn't help thinking of the way she looked without her clothes on, throwing back her head and spewing flames from her lips. "Hi," I said, "I was looking for Samantha? You know, *Jennifer*," I added, by way of assuring her I was on intimate terms here and not just some psychotic who'd managed to track them all down.

She didn't smile. Just gave me a look devoid of anything – love, hate, fear, interest, or even civility – turned her head away and shouted, "Sam! Sammy! It's for you!"

"Tell her it's Hart," I said, "she'll know who –" but I broke off because I was talking to myself: the doorway was empty. I could hear the jabber and squawk of the TV and the thump of bass-heavy music from one of the upstairs bedrooms, then a whisper of voices in the hall.

In the next moment a shadow fell across the plane of the open door, and Samantha slid into view, her face pale and tentative. "Oh," she said, and I could hear the relief in her voice. "Oh, hi."

"I've got something to tell you," I said, coming right out with it, "– bad news, I think. This woman just stopped me when I was pulling into the driveway

4 **to spew:** speien, spucken.
9f. **devoid of anything:** völlig ausdruckslos, leer.
10 **civility:** Höflichkeit.
15 **jabber** (coll.): Geplapper.
squawk: Kreischen.
16 **thump:** Dröhnen.
21 **tentative:** vorsichtig.

– my next-door neighbor – and they're circulating a petition." I watched her eyebrows, her eyes, saw the glint of the rings on her right hand as she swept it through her hair. "But I didn't sign. I blew her off."

She looked distracted, staring out over my shoulder as if she hadn't heard me. "Louis warned us there might be trouble," she said finally, "but it really isn't fair. I mean, do I look like some kind of slut to you? Do I?"

I wanted to make a speech, or at least a confession, and now was the time for it, now, but the best I could do was shake my head slowly and emphatically. *Louis?* Who was Louis?

Her eyes were burning. I heard a blast of gunfire from the TV, and then the volume went dead. "I'm sorry, Hart," Samantha said, lifting one bare foot from the floor to scratch the other with a long casual stroke of her instep, "but do you want to come in? You want a beer?"

And then I was in, following the sweep of Samantha's shoulders and hair and the sweet balsam scent of her into the living room I knew so well – and that was strange, surpassing strange, to know a place in its every apparent detail and yet never to have been there in the flesh. It was like a dream made concrete,

4 **I blew her off** (coll.): ich habe sie abgewimmelt.
5 **distracted:** abwesend, zerstreut.
8 **slut** (coll.): Schlampe.
14 **blast:** Explosion.
18 **instep:** Spann, Fußrücken.
23 **surpassing:** unvergleichlich, mehr als.

a vision come to life. I felt like a character in a play, walking onto the set for the first time – and I was, I *was*. Don't look at the camera, isn't that what they tell you on TV? I glanced up, and there it was, staring me in the face. Gina stuck her head through the swinging door to the kitchen. "Hi," she said, for form's sake, and then she disappeared – out onto the deck, I supposed, to tan her hot sexy young limbs. I sat in the chair facing the dead TV screen and Samantha went out of the frame and into the kitchen for the beer, and I couldn't help wondering how many hundreds of perverts went with her.

She came back with two beers and sat opposite me, in the armchair facing "Living Room Cam 2," and gave me a smile as she settled into the chair.

I took a sip of beer, smiled back, and said, "Who's Louis?"

Samantha was sitting with one leg tucked under her, her back arched, the beer pinioned between her legs. "He's one of the operators – of the site? He's got something like thirty of them around the country, and he's like –"

"A cyber-pimp?" It was out before I could think.

She frowned and looked down into the neck of the bottle a minute, then brought her head back up and flicked the hair out of her face. "I was going to say

6 **for form's sake:** der Form halber.
8 **to tan:** bräunen.
19 **to pinion:** umklammert halten.
23 **cyber-pimp:** Internetzuhälter.
24 **to frown:** die Stirn runzeln.

he's like used to this sort of thing, people hassling him over zoning laws and sex-oriented businesses and all that, but really, I mean, what's the big deal?"

"I watch," I said suddenly, looking directly into her eyes. "I watch you."

Her smile blossomed into a grin. "You do?"

I held her eyes. I nodded.

"Really? Well, that's – that's great. But you've never seen me do anything dirty, have you? Some of the girls get off on it, but I figure I'm just going to live, you know, and get my end out of it – it's a good deal. I need the money. I *like* the money. And if I'm nude in the shower or when I'm changing clothes and all these guys are jerking off or whatever, I don't care, that's life, you know what I mean?"

"You know when I like to watch you best? When you're asleep. You look so – I don't want to say angelic, but that's part of it – you just look so peaceful, I guess, and I feel like I'm right there with you, watching over you."

She got up from the chair then and crossed the room to me. "That's a sweet thing to say," she said, and she set her beer down on the coffee table and settled into the couch beside me. "Really sweet," she murmured, slipping an arm round my neck and bringing her face in for a close-up. Everything seemed

1 **to hassle:** schikanieren.
2 **zoning:** Zoneneinteilung.
3 **What's the big deal?** (coll.): Was soll denn das?; Na und?
10 **to get off on s.th.** (coll.): einen Kick bekommen von etwas.
14 **to jerk off** (coll.): sich einen runterholen.
26 **close-up:** Großaufnahme.

transformed in that moment, every object in the room coming into sudden focus, and I saw her with a deep and revelatory clarity. I kissed her. Felt the soft flutter of her lips and tongue against mine and forgot all about Stefania, my ex-wife, Sarah Schuster and Grandma Rivers. I broke away and then kissed her again, and it was a long, slow, sweet, lingering kiss and she was rubbing my back and I had my hands on her hips, just dreaming and dreaming. "Do you want to –?" I breathed. "Can you –?"

"Not here," she said, and she looked right into the camera. "They don't like it. They don't even like this."

"All right," I said, "all right," and I looked up too, right into the glassy eye of Camera 1. "What do we do now?"

"I don't know," she said. "Just hold me."

3 **revelatory clarity:** aufschlussreiche Klarheit.
7 **lingering:** ausgedehnt, lang.

Editorische Notiz

Der englische Text folgt den Ausgaben:

Descent of Man, Stories by T. Coraghessan Boyle, Boston/ Toronto: Little, Brown and Company, 1979 (*Heart of a Champion*).

T. Coraghessan Boyle, *Greasy Lake and Other Stories*, New York: Viking, 1985 (*Two Ships*).

If the River Was Whiskey, Stories by T. Coraghessan Boyle, New York: Viking, 1989 (*Sinking House*).

Without a Hero, Stories by T. Coraghessan Boyle, New York: Viking, 1994 (*Carnal Knowledge*).

T. Coraghessan Boyle, *After the Plague*, London: Bloomsbury, 2001 (*After the Plague, Peep Hall*).

Das Glossar erklärt in der Regel alle Wörter, die nicht im *Thematischen Grund- und Aufbauwortschatz Englisch* von Gernot Häublein und Recs Jenkins (Stuttgart/Düsseldorf/ Leipzig: Ernst Klett Verlag, 1993) verzeichnet sind. Die einzelnen Texte sind unabhängig voneinander glossiert, so dass jede Story für sich gelesen werden kann.

Im Glossar verwendete englische Abkürzungen

adv.	adverb
coll.	colloquial (umgangssprachlich)
fig.	figuratively (übertragen)
Fr.	French
Ital.	Italian

Mex. Span.	Mexican Spanish
o.s.	oneself
pej.	pejorative (abwertend)
pl.	plural
s.o.	someone
s.th.	something
vulg.	vulgar (vulgär, derb)

Literaturhinweise

I. Zu Autor und Werk

Adams, Elizabeth, »An Interview with T. Coraghessan Boyle«, in: *Chicago Review* 37 (1991), H. 2–3, S. 51–63.

Brussin, Alana, »Finishing What You've Started: An Interview with T. Coraghessan Boyle«, in: *Hayden's Ferry Review* 31 (2002) S. 135–147.

Raabe, David M., »Boyle's ›Descent of Man‹«, in: *Explicator* 58 (2000), H. 4, S. 223–226.

Schröder, Markus, *»Nice Guys Finish Last«: Sozialkritik in den Romanen T. Coraghessan Boyles*, Essen: Blaue Eule, 1997.

Spencer, Nicholas, »Inhuman(e) Subjects: Postmodern Theory and Contemporary Animal Liberation Fiction«, in: *From Virgin Land to Disney World: Nature and Its Discontents in the USA of Yesterday and Today*, hrsg. von Bernd Herzogenrath, Amsterdam: Rodopi, 2001, S. 187–208.

Vaid, Krishna Baldev, »Franz Kafka Writes to T. Coraghessan Boyle«, in: *Michigan Quarterly Review* 35 (1996), H. 3, S. 53–57.

Walker, Michael, »Boyle's ›Greasy Lake‹ and the Moral Failure of Postmodernism«, in: *Studies in Short Fiction* 31 (1994), H. 2, S. 247–255.

II. Internetseiten

http://www.tcboyle.com

Bei dieser sehr umfangreichen Internetseite handelt es sich um die offizielle Internetseite T. C. Boyles. Sie wird ständig aktualisiert, Boyle selbst liefert immer wieder kurze Beiträge und antwortet häufig sogar auf Fragen seiner internationalen Lesergemeinde. Zudem enthält die Seite umfangreiche Angaben zu Autor und Werk. Sämtliche bisher publizierten Romane und Kurzgeschichtensammlungen werden in Kurzkommentaren von Boyle selbst vorgestellt; hinzu kommen Textausschnitte, Rezensionen und Angaben zu Verfilmungen bzw. zu laufenden Verfilmungsprojekten. Als Volltexte stehen Interviews und ein autobiographischer Essay zur Verfügung, außerdem kann Boyles Lesung einer Kurzgeschichte gehört bzw. heruntergeladen werden.

http://www.tcboyle.net

Auch diese Seite bietet umfangreiches biographisches und bibliographisches Material zu Leben, Werk und Rezeption des Autors. Sie zeichnet sich insbesondere dadurch aus, dass sie etliche nicht-fiktionale Texte Boyles zugänglich macht, darunter Essays und Rezensionen.

http://www.tcboyle.de

Diese deutschsprachige Internet-Adresse bietet eine Vielzahl an ständig aktualisierten Informationen und stellt darüber hinaus ein Diskussionsforum für Leserinnen und Leser im deutschsprachigen Raum dar. Neben biographischen Angaben, Interviews, Rezensionen und Informationen zur Rezeption in Deutschland liefert sie bibliographische Angaben zu den Romanen und Kurzgeschichtensammlungen und ihren deutschen Übersetzungen. Für Lehrer gibt es eine Sammlung von Links zu Materialien unter der Rubrik „T C. Boyle für den Schulunterricht", die sich hauptsächlich auf den Roman *The Tortilla Curtain* beziehen.

http://www.englisch.schule.de/boyle/boyleaut.htm

Diese ebenfalls deutschsprachige Internet-Adresse (nicht nur) für Lehrer enthält viele weiterführende Links, die sich vor allem auf den Unterricht von *The Tortilla Curtain* beziehen. Einzusehen sind Informationen zum landeskundlichen Hintergrund und Unterrichtsentwürfe.

Nachwort

Satire, Ironie, Parodie – dies sind Begriffe, mit denen T. Coraghessan Boyles Texte, seine Kurzgeschichten wie seine Romane, wohl am häufigsten in Verbindung gebracht werden. Boyle, der oft als »enfant terrible« der zeitgenössischen amerikanischen Literaturszene beschrieben worden ist – wobei sich diese Bezeichnung nicht nur auf seine Texte, sondern gerade auch auf seine Biographie und auf sein ab und an exzentrisches Auftreten bezogen hat –, schreibt rasant, amüsant und zumeist auch provokant. Seine literarischen Auseinandersetzungen mit einer Vielzahl an historischen wie zeitgenössischen Stoffen, vor allem der zielsichere Blick für – oft alltägliche – Situationen, in denen sich zentrale Themen und Konflikte der amerikanischen Gesellschaft offenbaren, machen seine Texte zur lesenswerten, stets unterhaltsamen wie auch im besten Sinne des Wortes irritierenden Lektüre.

Thomas John Boyle wurde 1948 in Peekskill, New York, geboren. Seinen zweiten Familiennamen Coraghessan, den irische Vorfahren trugen, nahm er in den 1960er-Jahren während seiner Zeit auf dem College an. Boyle wuchs in einer katholisch geprägten Familie auf, seine Kindheit und Jugend waren von der Alkoholabhängigkeit beider Eltern geprägt. Um der Einberufung in die Armee – und damit einem Einsatz in Vietnam – zu entgehen, nahm er nach dem College-Abschluss eine Stelle als Lehrer an einer Schule in einem sozialen Brennpunkt an, war jedoch von der Aufgabe schnell überfordert und glitt in die Drogenabhängigkeit ab. Während der Ausbildung begann er, Kurzgeschichten zu schreiben, und diese offenbar zumindest teilweise therapeutisch wirkende Aktivität sollte dazu beitragen, dass es ihm gelang, seinem Leben eine neue Richtung zu geben. 1972 veröffentlichte er seine erste Kurzgeschichte und erhielt dadurch Einlass in den renommierten Writers' Workshop an der Iowa State University, wo er bei so bekannten Schriftstellern wie

John Cheever und John Irving studierte. Mitte der 70er-Jahre machte er seine Universitätsabschlüsse, u. a. promovierte er 1977 mit einer Reihe von Kurzgeschichten, die im Jahr 1979 unter dem Titel *Descent of Man* veröffentlicht wurden. Seit dieser Zeit arbeitet Boyle nicht nur als Autor, sondern auch als Professor für Creative Writing an der University of Southern California. Heute lebt er mit seiner Frau und seinen drei Kindern bei Santa Barbara in Kalifornien.

Seit der Publikation seiner ersten Geschichte im Jahre 1972 veröffentlichte Boyle zehn Romane, sieben Geschichten-Sammlungen (die zusammen 82 Geschichten enthalten) sowie etliche weitere Geschichten, die einzeln in verschiedenen Zeitschriften erschienen sind. In vielen dieser Geschichten äußert sich ein ausgeprägtes Interesse an Phänomenen der amerikanischen, massenmedial geprägten Populärkultur. Zusammen mit der parodistischen Schreibweise und der die Aufmerksamkeit auf sich ziehenden sprachlich-stilistischen Gestaltung seiner Texte zeigt sich darin ein Schreiben im Zeichen der Postmoderne. Seit den politischen, künstlerischen und medialen Umbrüchen der 1950er- und 60er-Jahre spiegelt sich in der Literatur – wie auch im Film, in der Kunst und in der Architektur – ein verstärktes, als postmodern bezeichnetes Interesse an der gesellschaftlichen Relevanz von Populärkultur und Massenmedien, an der Rolle von Sprache und Texten für Prozesse der individuellen wie kollektiven Sinn- und Identitätsstiftung. Boyles erfinderischer und ideenreicher Stil, sein Sprachwitz, sein versierter Umgang mit unterschiedlichen sprachlichen Niveaus – von der Umgangssprache über die formelhafte Sprache der Medien wie der Politik bis hin zu Aspekten von Fachsprachen – und schließlich der kritische Dialog mit einer Vielzahl an Vorgängertexten zeugen somit nicht nur von stilistischer Vielschichtigkeit, sondern auch von dem Bemühen, die Aufmerksamkeit auf die kulturell formative Rolle von Sprache und Texten zu lenken.

Boyle spricht in Interviews immer wieder davon, dass es ihm bei seinem Schreiben darum gehe, zu entdecken und zu erforschen. Sein Ziel ist es, komplexen, manchmal sogar paradox erscheinenden Sachverhalten auf den Grund zu gehen. Gegenstand seines schriftstellerischen Interesses ist dabei oft die zeitgenössische amerikanische Gesellschaft, deren politischen und kulturellen Ausprägungen er sich in durchaus gesellschaftskritischer Absicht nähert – allerdings aus der Perspektive des Satirikers, der inszeniert und irritiert und nicht mit dem moralischen Zeigefinger operiert. Als besonders geeignet für diese Art schriftstellerischen Erforschens etwa von Phänomenen der Konsumgesellschaft oder auch der amerikanischen Umweltschutzbewegung erweist sich dabei die Perspektive derer, die am Rande der Gesellschaft stehen oder abrupt aus einem gesellschaftlich etablierten, rollenkonformen Alltag gerissen werden und sich unversehens in ungewohnten Situationen wiederfinden. In Boyles Außenseiter- und Sonderlingsfiguren und in seinen ab und an absurd anmutenden Handlungsverläufen zeigen sich die klassischen Mittel satirischen Schreibens: Übertreibung und drastische Zuspitzung. Sie werden genutzt, um Gewohntes – tradierte Haltungen, Denkweisen und Erklärungsmuster – in Frage zu stellen und neue Einsichten zu ermöglichen.

»Heart of a Champion«

Die Hinwendung zu Formen der Populärkultur und die Beschäftigung mit dem Einfluss der Massenmedien zeigen sich deutlich gleich in der ersten Geschichte der vorliegenden Sammlung. *Heart of a Champion* spielt auf die von 1957 bis 1964 produzierten Lassie-Fernsehfilme an, in denen der bis heute wohl bekannteste Leinwand-Hund dem Farmerjungen Timmy Martin gehört. Boyle nutzt hier einen Ich-Erzähler, der sich an eindrückliche Szenen und an den typischen Handlungsverlauf der vielen Episoden dieser Fernsehserie erinnert: an die Farm und ihre Umgebung, in der Timmy und seine Eltern leben, und an die Abenteuer, die der Junge mit seiner Hündin Lassie erlebt. Die Geschichte setzt sich aus einzelnen Vignetten zusammen, die als stark visuell geprägte Erinnerungsfragmente vom Erzähler aneinandergereiht werden und die zunächst den typischen Verlauf dieser Abenteuer skizzieren. Da sich Lassie als »champion« – als heldenhaft, klug, geschickt und dem Menschen gegenüber absolut loyal agierend – erweist, gehen Timmy und sie aus noch so gefährlichen Situationen immer heil hervor. Im Zuge des Erzählens entwickelt sich dann jedoch eine überraschende Handlungsdynamik, die das typische Muster unterläuft. Es ist »das Herz« dieser heldenhaften Hündin, das ein weiteres Abenteuer einen ungewohnten Verlauf nehmen lässt. Lassie, deren Geschlecht in den Fernsehfilmen so gut wie keine Rolle spielt, erweist sich als Hundedame, die einem räudigen Koyoten verfällt, ihre Loyalität Timmy gegenüber aufgibt und ihn in einer lebensbedrohlichen Situation seinem Schicksal überlässt – der Junge liegt bewusstlos unter einem umgestürzten Baum, und zwar in einem Tal, das in Kürze von Wassermassen überschwemmt zu werden droht. Diese Parodie des typischen Handlungsverlaufs zieht vor allem eine zentrale Aussage der Fernsehserie in Zweifel, nämlich die Möglichkeit einer ländlich-pastoralen Lebensweise, die ihre ideale Ausprägung in der Existenz des Farmers und seiner Familie findet.

Das Ideal einer pastoralen Existenz spielt für die Formierung eines amerikanischen nationalen Selbstbildes seit den ersten Dekaden nach der Staatsgründung Ende des 18. Jahrhunderts eine bedeutende Rolle. In Thomas Jeffersons *Notes on the State of Virginia* (1784) und Hector St. John de Crèvecœurs *Letters from an American Farmer* (1782), zwei ›klassischen‹, kulturell prägenden Texten der frühen amerikanischen Literatur, wird der amerikanische Farmer als ein Modell-Amerikaner entworfen, dessen Arbeit mit dem Land und dessen enger Kontakt zur Natur, zur Tier- und Pflanzenwelt, ihn zu einem moralisch besseren Wesen machen. Vor dem Hintergrund der immer massiver einsetzenden Urbanisierung und Industrialisierung im 19. Jahrhundert entstand eine Vision amerikanisch-pastoraler Existenz, die im Farmer und seiner Familie – frei von den korrumpierenden Einflüssen des wesentlich komplexeren Lebens in den rasch anwachsenden Städten – die moralische Keimzelle der Nation erkannte. Die Farm wurde zu jenem Ort, an dem immer neue Generationen von Amerikanern die moralischen Grundwerte des Landes erlernen und einüben konnten. Bis heute ist dieses pastorale Ideal ein wichtiger Faktor individueller wie kollektiver amerikanischer Identitätsbildung: die Filmgattung des Western, unzählige Fernsehserien (neben *Lassie* etwa auch *Little House on the Prairie*, dt. *Unsere kleine Farm*), aber auch die Selbststilisierung etlicher amerikanischer Präsidenten (man denke an den ›Erdnussfarmer‹ Jimmy Carter, an den ›Cowboy‹ Ronald Reagan oder auch an den ›Texas-Rancher‹ George W. Bush) können als kulturelle Manifestationen dieses Ideals gelten. Die Figur des Timmy steht zudem beispielhaft für eine lange Reihe amerikanischer fiktionaler Gestalten, die ihre Initiation in eine pastorale Lebensweise und das damit verbundene Wertesystem erfährt. Das wohl bekannteste Beispiel ist hier Mark Twains Figur des Tom Sawyer.

Mit *Heart of a Champion* zitiert Boyle somit eine schier unübersehbare Menge an – medial unterschiedlich konkretisierten – Texten an, rückt deren kulturell prägende Kraft ins Blickfeld und hinterfragt gleichzeitig die Gültigkeit des pastoralen Ideals. Von zentraler Bedeutung ist dabei die Tatsache, dass die Hündin Lassie ihre Loyalität dem Menschen gegenüber aufkündigt und ihren Instinkten folgt. Diese Wendung der Geschichte entlarvt das pastorale Ideal zum einen als ein ausschließlich anthropozentrisches, auf die Bedürfnisse und den Machtwillen des Menschen ausgerichtetes und zum andern als ein theoretisches Konstrukt, das die konkretsinnliche Dimension aller Erfahrung völlig außer Acht lässt. In der Fernsehserie werden die Bedürfnisse der Hündin, ihre auf Selbsterhalt und eigene Bedürfnisbefriedigung ausgerichteten Instinkte unterschlagen, die Darstellung des Hundes reflektiert statt dessen einzig den menschlichen Wunsch nach totaler Zuwendung und Verfügbarkeit. Mit Lassies instinktgetriebener Liebe zum Koyoten rücken die im pastoralen Ideal weitgehend ausgeblendete körperlich-sinnliche Dimension von Erfahrung sowie die Rolle der Sexualität in den Vordergrund. Während in den ersten Vignetten der Geschichte jeglicher Hinweis auf Sinneswahrnehmungen fehlt – Schmerz und daraus abzuleitende Furcht etwa spielen in den zunächst beschriebenen Abenteuern keine Rolle –, kommen diese mit dem Auftauchen des Koyoten immer stärker zum Tragen und werden als entscheidendes Defizit des Ideals erkennbar. So erweist sich die modellhafte Farmerfamilie Martin etwa als überaus prüde, als die Eltern Timmy nicht erklären, dass er offenbar Lassie bei der Paarung mit dem Koyoten beobachtet hat.

Boyles Wahl eines rückblickend erzählenden Ich-Erzählers, der immer von »wir« spricht, deutet an, dass dessen Lassie-Reminiszenzen nicht nur von individueller, sondern von überindividueller Bedeutung sind. Sie suggeriert, dass nicht nur der Erzähler, sondern eine ganze Fernseh-Generation von dieser Serie beeinflusst wurde, von den Werten und Normen, die ihre Bilder und Handlungsentwürfe zum Ausdruck bringen. Das Fernsehen wird als Medium vorgestellt, dessen Botschaften individuelle wie kollektive Selbstbilder prägen. Allerdings zeigt sich dabei auch, dass dieser Einfluss der kritischen Hinterfragung standhalten muss. Schon bevor sich der Ich-Erzähler dem Sog des typischen Handlungsmusters entzieht und es quasi auf den Kopf stellt, kommt es bei seinem Bemühen um detailgetreue Wiedergabe der erinnerten Bilder und Geschichten zu Irritationen. Es fallen ihm zunehmend unrealistische Einzelheiten der Darstellung auf. Mehrfach kommentiert er z. B. die Künstlichkeit von Timmys Frisur oder auch die Tatsache, dass die Augen des Hundes offenbar mit Mascara geschminkt wurden, um einen stärkeren Effekt beim Zuschauer zu erzielen. Die Bewertung solcher Erinnerungsbilder weisen den Ich-Erzähler als kritischen

Fernseh-Konsumenten aus, der die Botschaften des Films, die in Figurenzeichnung und Handlungsverlauf ausgedrückten Ideen und Werte, nicht einfach übernimmt, sondern im Abgleich mit anderen Erfahrungen zu überprüfen und in Frage zu stellen vermag.

Die letzte Vignette der Geschichte fügt der Auseinandersetzung mit der identitätsstiftenden Kraft des Mediums Fernsehen eine letzte, zusätzliche Dimension hinzu. Hier kommt es ein weiteres Mal zu einer verblüffenden Wendung innerhalb der Handlungsdynamik. Entgegen dem Verlauf des letzten Abenteuers, das eindeutig auf Timmys Ertrinken und Tod zusteuert, zeichnet der letzte Abschnitt nämlich völlig unvermittelt erneut ein pastoral-friedliches Bild. Der Erzähler präsentiert Szenen aus der für die Serie typischen ersten Filmsequenz, in der Timmy Lassie durch ein Weizenfeld in der Sommersonne auf ihn zulaufen sieht. Dieses Ende der Geschichte kann einerseits als ultimatives erzählerisches Mittel begriffen werden, mit dem Boyle die vom Fernsehen geschaffene pastorale Realität ad absurdum führt. Andererseits jedoch lässt es sich auch als Hinweis auf die trotz allem immense, nicht so leicht außer Kraft zu setzende Suggestivkraft des medial inszenierten pastoralen Realitätsentwurfs lesen. Dem kritischen Fernseh-Konsumenten wird sein Alter Ego entgegengesetzt, das dem Wunsch nach einem »happy ending«, der Befriedigung des Bedürfnisses nach dem pastoralen Familienidyll, nachgibt. Die Auseinandersetzung mit der Rolle des Mediums Fernsehen lässt somit keinen Zweifel daran, dass es eine realitäts- und identitätsstiftende Kraft ausübt, es bleibt jedoch offen, wie stark diese Kraft ist.

»Two Ships«

Die Handlung der Geschichte *Two Ships* kreist um einen Akt des Verrats, der zum einen den endgültigen Niedergang einer Jugendfreundschaft besiegelt, zum anderen aber auch eine kritische Auseinandersetzung mit dem materialistischen, konsumorientierten Lebensstil der amerikanischen Mittelklasse darstellt. Gegenstand ist der Konflikt zwischen zwei ehemaligen Freunden, die zusammen aufwuchsen, während ihrer Teenager-Zeit in den späten 60er- und 70er-Jahren gemeinsam gegen ihr bürgerliches Elternhaus rebellierten, deren Wege sich danach jedoch trennten. Den einen, Casper R. Hansen, führt sein Weg in die weitere politische Radikalisierung. Dem Verteilen von marxistisch inspirierten Flugblättern während der Schulzeit folgen nach Abbruch der College-Ausbildung eine kurze Zeit als revolutionärer Arbeiter, die Einberufung zum Militär in der Zeit des Vietnamkriegs, die fast sofortige Desertierung sowie Aufenthalte im Ausland, die sämtlich im Zeichen radikal linker, anti-kapitalistischer politischer Agitation stehen. Der andere, der Ich-Erzähler Jack, kehrt auf die Bahn einer geordneten Mittelklasse-Existenz zurück. Er studiert, wird Anwalt, heiratet, gründet eine Familie und lebt bei Einsetzen der Handlung in materiell recht komfortablen Umständen. Aus diesen reißt ihn eine Beobachtung, mit der die Geschichte einsetzt: Auf dem Weg zum Tennisplatz nimmt er vom Auto aus mit Schrecken wahr, dass Casper nach zwölfjähriger Abwesenheit wieder aufgetaucht ist und die Straße entlanggeht. Dieser Schrecken entsteht nicht so sehr deshalb, weil ihm klar wird, dass seine und Caspers extrem unterschiedliche Lebensweisen ein beträchtliches Konfliktpotenzial bergen, sondern er gründet in seiner Erinnerung an einen Verrat. Jack hatte etwa ein Jahr zuvor einem FBI-Beamten gegenüber eine Aussage gemacht, die für Casper die Zwangseinweisung in eine psychiatrische Klinik bedeutete. Nach Caspers Geisteszustand befragt, erklärt Jack den ehemaligen Freund für geistig schwer beeinträchtigt. Der Befragung durch den FBI-Mann war ein Telefonat vorausgegangen, in dem Casper Jack anflehte, seinen psychischen Zustand als völlig normal zu beschreiben, sollte er befragt werden. Casper war zu diesem Zeitpunkt offenbar bewusst, dass staatliche Polizeiorgane einen Weg suchten, des unbequemen Linken habhaft zu werden.

Die kritische Auseinandersetzung mit dem materialistischen, karriere- und konsumorientierten Lebensstil der amerikanischen Mittelklasse manifestiert sich nicht allein im offen-politischen Widerstand Caspers, sondern vor allem auch in den Haltungen und Handlungen des Erzählers Jack. Wie schon in *Heart of a Champion* nutzt Boyle auch hier einen Ich-Erzähler als Fokalisierungsinstanz, d. h., es sind allein Jacks Wahrnehmungen, Gedanken und Erinnerungen, aus denen sich die Geschichte aufbaut und die eine Einschätzung der Situation und ihrer Hintergründe liefern. Das auffälligste stilistische Merkmal, das Jacks Erzählen auszeichnet, ist dabei der von Erschrecken, Angst, Ärger und Trotz gekennzeichnete Ton. Erschrecken, ja Panik, und ein Gefühl der Atemlosigkeit, das seinen beginnenden Verfolgungswahn begleitet, werden gleich im ersten Absatz der Geschichte erzeugt: Dem ersten Satz – »I saw him today« (S. 22) –, der den Moment des Wiedererkennens markiert, folgen knappe, abrupt aneinandergefügte Satzfragmente, die Jacks Wahrnehmungen zum Ausdruck bringen und gleichzeitig signalisieren, wie schwer es ihm fällt, sich in seiner plötzlich fundamental veränderten Situation zurechtzufinden. Das Tempo, das ein solches Erzählen in kurzen Sätzen und Satzfragmenten erzeugt, und der Effekt der Verwirrung, der durch das rasche Aneinanderreihen diverser Sinneswahrnehmungen oder auch Erinnerungsbilder entsteht, werden im weiteren Verlauf der Geschichte von Boyle immer wieder genutzt, um den Handlungshöhepunkt, das Treffen von Jack und Casper, atmosphärisch vorzubereiten.

Vor allem Jacks komplexe Gefühlslage und einige wesentliche Informationen, die in seinen Erinnerungen auftauchen, dienen nun der Einschätzung dieser Figur, die als Repräsentant der wohlhabenden amerikanischen Mittelklasse zu sehen ist. In seinem Ärger über Casper und in seinem trotzigen Beharren auf den Entscheidungen, die sein Leben geprägt haben, drückt sich eine durchaus berechtigte Abwehr der von Casper gelebten Radikalität aus. Der Wunsch, sich eine berufliche und familiäre Existenz aufzubauen, wird an sich nicht kritisiert. In seiner Angst und Panik jedoch zeigt sich Jacks latentes Schuldbewusstsein, sein schlechtes Gewissen angesichts des Verrats und der gravierenden Folgen, die dieser für Casper hatte. Nicht seine Entscheidung für ein angepasstes Leben, sondern die Tatsache, dass er seinen Lebensstandard und seine Karriere auf Kosten eines andern zu sichern versucht hat, sind kritikwürdig. Verstärkt wird diese Bewertung zusätzlich durch den Fall, den er in der Kanzlei gerade betreut. Seine Aufgabe besteht darin, für einen Klienten – einen Industriellen, der Batterien produziert und offenbar Giftmüll in den Hudson River eingeleitet hat – Lücken in der bestehenden Umweltgesetzgebung zu finden, um so eine Bestrafung zu verhindern. Die Tatsache, dass Jack sich dieser Aufgabe ohne moralische Skrupel zu widmen begonnen hat, nimmt ihm jegliche Integrität und entlarvt ihn als einen Menschen, der privat wie beruflich rücksichtslos agiert und nur auf sein eigenes Vorankommen bedacht ist.

Auch die Figur Casper weist Ambivalenzen auf, die Boyle bereits durch die Wahl seines Namens signalisiert. Der Name Casper deutet auf die Figur des Narren hin, der in einer langen literarischen Tradition einerseits als törichter Narr die Dummheiten und Fehler des Menschen verkörperte, andererseits aber auch als weiser Narr den Menschen ihre Dummheiten und Fehler aufzuzeigen vermochte. Als töricht kann Casper insofern eingeschätzt werden, als er durch seine Unbedingtheit, die keine andere Existenzweise anerkennt, seinen Mitmenschen zu viel abverlangt. Als weise kann demgegenüber sein Einsatz gegen soziale Ungerechtigkeit und gegen Kriege, die hegemonialen politischen und wirtschaftlichen Zwecken dienen, bewertet werden. Casper provoziert, hinterfragt und entlarvt den egoistischen Konformismus Jacks. Über die Figur Casper positioniert Boyle seine Geschichte somit in die lange Tradition der satirischen Narrenliteratur, deren Zweck immer darin lag, menschliche Schwächen wie auch gesellschaftliche Missstände aufzuzeigen. Zudem deutet dieser Gattungsbezug auch eine mögliche Interpretation des Titels an. Die beiden Schiffe, von denen darin die Rede ist, können als Anspielung auf eines der üblichen Narrenfahrzeuge gedeutet werden, nämlich das »Narrenschiff«, das menschliche Schwächen und Torheiten ausstellt.

Der Kontext der Narrenliteratur wirft schließlich auch ein Schlaglicht darauf, wie in der Geschichte die Relevanz der Jugendprotestkultur der 60er- und 70er-Jahre eingeschätzt wird. In den Figuren Jack und Casper deuten sich unterschiedliche Motivationen an, die diese Bewegung geprägt haben mögen. Jack erscheint als unpolitischer Jugendlicher, dem es bei Sabotageakten vor allem um das Aufbegehren gegen die väterliche Autorität, um Nervenkitzel und Abenteuer geht und dessen spätere Rückkehr in rollenkonformes Mittelklasse-Verhalten durchaus konsequent ist. In Casper manifestiert sich der extrem politisierte Jugendliche, dessen Prinzipien ihn kompromisslos werden lassen und in die Radikalität treiben. Werden Jack und Casper als Repräsentanten der Jugendprotestkultur angesehen, so suggeriert ihr Werdegang ein gehöriges Maß an ›Torheit‹: Die Unfähigkeit, miteinander zu kommunizieren, und schließlich der Verrat, den der gesellschaftlich Arrivierte am andern begeht, markieren das Vergeben der Chancen des politischen Protests der 60er- und 70er-Jahre.

»Sinking House«

Die gesellschaftskritische Dimension, die sich auf Facetten des Lebensstils und der Werte der alles in allem gutsituierten amerikanischen Mittelklasse bezieht, kennzeichnet auch die Geschichte *Sinking House*. Deren Handlung vollzieht sich in einem kalifornischen Vorort. Das zentrale Ereignis, das sie in

Gang setzt, ist die Reaktion einer alten Frau, Muriel Burgess, auf den Tod ihres Ehemannes, Monty. Muriel öffnet sämtliche Wasserhähne in Haus und Garten und setzt das Grundstück damit unter Wasser. Als das Wasser auch das Nachbargrundstück erreicht und sogar in das Nachbarhaus einzudringen beginnt, werden Meg und Sonny Terwilliger, ein junges Ehepaar, er Immobilienmakler, sie Hausfrau und Mutter einer kleinen Tochter, aktiv. Sie versuchen, etwas gegen diese Überflutung zu unternehmen. Da es ihnen jedoch nicht gelingt, Muriel zum Schließen der Hähne zu bewegen, veranlassen sie deren Abholung durch die Polizei. Das Ende der Geschichte deutet die Einweisung Muriels in eine Anstalt an.

Wie im Falle des Erzählers Jack in *Two Ships* wird auch hier die geordnete Existenz einer Familie, die der Terwilligers, massiv gestört. Muriels Verhalten widerspricht allen üblichen Verhaltensmustern, und die allmähliche Überflutung von Häusern und Grundstücken signalisiert eine zunehmend unerträgliche Anarchie. In Gefahr gerät zunächst der materielle Besitz der Terwilligers. Der Garten beginnt sich in einen Sumpf zu verwandeln, im Haus leiden die Fußböden. Da Dinge einen ausgesprochen hohen Stellenwert im Leben von Meg und Sonny einnehmen, reagieren beide sofort alarmiert – in der Geschichte wird der Beschreibung der Ausstattung ihres Hauses, von Schuhen und Kleidung auffällig viel Raum gegeben, es wird etliche Male darauf verwiesen, wie wichtig der Besitz von teuren Markenartikeln für die beiden ist. Dies erklärt, warum sehr schnell auch ihr seelisches Gleichgewicht in Gefahr gerät. Materieller Besitz als Ausdruck beruflichen wie sozialen Erfolgs stellt für beide den zentralen identitätsstiftenden Faktor dar. Der scheinbare Angriff auf das materielle Eigentum kommt einem Angriff auf die eigene Identität gleich. In der Reaktion der Terwilligers, in den unkontrollierten, panikartig anmutenden Wutausbrüchen Sonnys, aber auch im teilweise apathisch wirkenden Verhalten Megs, zeigt sich die Anfälligkeit einer so fundierten Identität.

Sinking House unterzieht das amerikanische Ideal des

»suburbian way of life«, des Lebens im Vorort großer städtischer Zentren, wie es sich seit den 1950er-Jahren entwickelt hat, einem kritischen Blick. Dabei zeigt sich, dass Ideal und Wirklichkeit weit auseinanderklaffen. Haus und Garten mögen einen angemessen hohen sozialen Status suggerieren, das soziale Zusammenleben jedoch ist von Isolation und Desinteresse gekennzeichnet: Der Tod eines Nachbarn wird erst dann bemerkt, als der eigene Besitz in Gefahr gerät; die Hintergründe unüblichen Verhaltens interessieren weder Nachbarn noch Polizei. Niemand, weder Meg oder Sonny noch die Polizei, versucht, Muriels Verhalten zu ergründen. Niemand erfährt somit, dass das Aufdrehen der Wasserhähne ein Reinigungsritual darstellt, dass es spontaner Ausdruck eines Gefühls der Befreiung aus der schier unerträglichen Phase der letzten Jahre ihrer Ehe ist, die vom physischen wie psychischen Missbrauch durch den kranken Monty geprägt war. Niemand erfährt, dass das Wasser ständig laufen muss, weil Monty für Muriel noch immer quälend präsent ist. Sobald die Hähne abgedreht sind, kann sie seine Präsenz fühlen und ist dem Horror erneut ausgesetzt. In all dem zeigt sich die Kehrseite der amerikanischen Konsumgesellschaft.

Eine Verdichtung der Problematik ergibt sich durch ein von Boyle gespanntes Netz an Parallelen zwischen den Figuren. Zunächst ist hierbei auf die Wahl der Erzählperspektiven zu verweisen. Boyle nutzt einen auktorialen Erzähler, wählt als zentrale Fokalisierungsinstanzen jedoch die Figuren Muriel und Meg. In den sechs Teilen, in die die Geschichte gegliedert ist, entwickeln sich die Ereignisse abwechselnd in den Wahrnehmungen und Gedanken der beiden Frauen. Dabei entstehen eindringliche Psychogramme, die eine zunächst nicht vermutete Parallelität der Erfahrungen andeuten. Es zeigt sich, dass die Verhältnisse zwischen den Ehepartnern von sehr ähnlicher Natur sind, dass Meg auf dem besten Wege ist, dieselben Erfahrungen wie Muriel zu machen. Der Text suggeriert dies in den sehr ähnlich klingenden Namen »Monty« und »Sonny« und in Passagen, in denen Muriel in ihrem Nachbarn Sonny Züge ihres verstorbenen Mannes erkennt. Sonny teilt mit Monty die Eigenschaft, schnell reizbar zu sein und unverhältnismäßig brutal zu reagieren. Als er zum ersten Mal das Ausmaß der Überschwemmung im Garten erkennt, stürmt er zur Tür des Nachbarhauses und schlägt dagegen »wie die Gestapo« – dieser drastische Vergleich signalisiert jenen Grad an Unbeherrschtheit, der auch Monty während seiner letzten Lebensjahre kennzeichnete. Bezeichnend ist, dass in der anschließenden Passage Meg Sonnys wütenden Blick auf sich bezieht. Sie begreift, dass er sie für die Situation verantwortlich machen will, und angesichts seiner ungezügelten Wut steigt Furcht in ihr auf. Diese Furcht ähnelt der Furcht, die Muriel Monty gegenüber auszuhalten hatte. Meg verspürt hinsichtlich der Handlungen Muriels von Anfang an eine gewisse Faszination, und ihre letzten Aktionen vermitteln den Eindruck, dass sie zu ahnen beginnt, wie ähnlich ihrer beider Lebensgeschichten werden könnten. Sie begibt sich an den Ort, den Muriel und Monty bewohnt haben, und will »nachfühlen«, wie sich Muriel gefühlt haben mag. Die Geschichte lässt offen, welche Folgen sich aus Megs Ahnungen ergeben könnten.

Die Verschränkung der (potenziellen) Erfahrungen Muriels und Megs rückt die Bedeutung von Häusern ein letztes Mal in den Mittelpunkt und erlaubt eine Deutung des Titels der Geschichte, die weit über das beschriebene konkrete Problem hinausgeht. Es sind nicht nur die Häuser der Burgess' und der Terwilligers, die in einem Sumpf zu versinken drohen, sondern auch die ›Idee‹ des Hauses als Zentrum menschlichen Lebens, als Mikrokosmos, der auch gesamtgesellschaftliches Zusammenleben ordnet und strukturiert. Die »versinkenden Häuser« symbolisieren eine ›versinkende‹, in hohem Maße patriarchal und materialistisch fundierte Zivilisation.

»Carnal Knowledge«

In *Carnal Knowledge* befasst sich Boyle mit einer Thematik, die auch in vielen anderen seiner Texte – in Kurzgeschichten wie Romanen – zum Tragen kommt, nämlich mit dem Thema Umwelt- und Naturschutz. In diesem Falle geht es um den moralisch angemessenen Umgang des Menschen mit Tieren, um das Problem der Massentierhaltung und um den radikalen Tierschutz. Die im Raum Los Angeles angesiedelte Handlung ist vor dem Hintergrund der Aktionen verschiedener radikaler Umweltschutzorganisationen zu sehen, die seit den 1970er-Jahren vor allem an der amerikanischen Westküste, im umweltpolitisch engagiertesten Teil der USA, aktiv sind und mit ihren z. T. spektakulären Sabotage-Aktionen immer wieder für Aufsehen sorgen. Erneut lotet die Geschichte die Diskrepanz zwischen einem Ideal und seiner konkreten Umsetzung aus, hier geht es um das Ideal einer der Würde nicht nur des Menschen, sondern auch der Tiere verpflichteten Gesellschaft, wie es von der zeitgenössischen Tierschutzbewegung postuliert wird.

Wieder arbeitet Boyle mit einem Ich-Erzähler, Jim, der allerdings kein Familienvater und Karrieretyp wie Jack in *Two Ships* und Sonny in *Sinking House* ist, sondern ein etwa dreißigjähriger Junggeselle, Werbetexter mit wenig ausgeprägten Karriereambitionen, aber durchaus darauf bedacht, sich das Leben angenehm und interessant zu gestalten. Rückblickend, und z. T. in bitter ironischem Ton, erzählt Jim von seiner kurzen Affäre mit der Tierschützerin Alena Jorgensen. Er erzählt, wie ihn seine »Fleischeslust« – sein »carnal knowledge« –, sein vor allem sexuell begründetes Verlangen nach Alena vorübergehend zum Teil der radikalen Tierschutzbewegung werden lässt. Zu Jims Erlebnissen gehören die Teilnahme an einer Protestdemonstration vor einem Pelzladen, die darin endet, dass er brutal zusammengeschlagen wird, sowie die Beteiligung an einer Truthahn-Befreiungsaktion kurz vor Thanksgiving, jenem amerikanischen

Feiertag, an dem in Erinnerung an die erste Ernte der englischen Einwanderer zu Beginn des 17. Jahrhunderts traditionell ein Truthahn verzehrt wird. Jim, Alena und der den Tierschutz professionell betreibende Rolfe befreien in einer Nacht-und-Nebel-Aktion Hunderte von Truthähnen – die allerdings auf ihrer Flucht nicht allzu weit kommen. Am nächsten Tag muss Jim auf der Fahrt zurück nach Hause feststellen, dass die verängstigten Tiere nach ihrer Flucht aus den Ställen geradewegs auf eine Autobahn gerieten, wo sie fast alle vom rollenden Verkehr erfasst und getötet wurden. Spätestens zu diesem Zeitpunkt muss dem Leser oder der Leserin deutlich werden, dass Boyle mit Jim eine Art Anti-Helden geschaffen hat, dessen z. T. grotesk anmutende Erfahrungen als temporäres Mitglied der radikalen Tierschutzbewegung große Zweifel aufkommen lassen, ob deren Aktionen tatsächlich als moralisch vorbildlich oder gar heldenhaft angesehen werden können.

Jims Bericht zieht die Anliegen der Tierschützer keineswegs generell in Zweifel. Über Strategien der Sympathielenkung wird z. B. die Tierquälerei in Versuchslaboren der Kosmetikindustrie eindringlich kritisiert. So schließt Jim mit dem Hund Alf Frieden, nachdem er die Geschichte seiner Misshandlung gehört hat, obwohl die Umstände ihres Kennenlernens unangenehme waren – Alf hatte ihn angepinkelt. Kritik am Tragen von Pelzen, da deren industrielle Herstellung die Tötung einer immensen Zahl an Tieren erfordert, wird durch die Prügel, die Jim am Ende des Protesttages bezieht, zum Ausdruck gebracht. Und die zu einem Gemetzel führende Befreiung der Truthähne, die in industrieller Massentierhaltung im Zeichen ökonomischer Gewinnmaximierung gezüchtet werden, fordert letztlich dazu auf, diese verdeckte Dimension eines der wichtigsten Feiertage der USA zumindest wahrzunehmen und sich klarzumachen, dass der Preis des Feierns nationaler Identität in der millionenfachen Mästung und Massenschlachtung von Tieren besteht.

Während die Anliegen der Tierschützer somit bestätigt

werden, werden ihre Motivation und ihre Ideologie gehörig in Zweifel gezogen. Mit satirischen Mitteln zeichnet Boyle dabei zwei Extremtypen des radikalen Tierschützers: den, der aus völlig anderen Motiven handelt, und den, dessen Aktionen in hohem Maße in einer quasi-fundamentalistischen Ablehnung jener Spezies gründet, die – evolutionär betrachtet – auch zu den Tieren zählt: in der Ablehnung der Spezies Mensch. Den ersten Typ verkörpert der Erzähler Jim. Schon im ersten Teil der Geschichte wird klar, dass ihm Umwelt- oder auch Tierschutzideale völlig fremd sind und dass ihn letztlich allein sexuelle Anziehung antreibt. Bevor Jim Alena trifft, verbringt er seinen Geburtstagsnachmittag mit dem Lesen von Ökothrillern am Strand, Naturlandschaft wie fiktionale ökologische Apokalypse dienen gleichermaßen der Entspannung und Unterhaltung. Im letzten Teil zeigt sich, dass selbst die intensive Konfrontation mit der Tierschutzproblematik während seiner Teilnahme an den Protestaktionen daran nichts geändert hat: Gierig und voller Vorfreude sehnt er sich nach seinen Tagen der Abstinenz einem Fleischgericht entgegen. Den Typ des fundamentalistischen Tierschützers verkörpern Alena und Rolfe. Obwohl Alenas Motivation glaubwürdig erscheint – sie hat ihr Veterinärstudium an den Nagel gehängt, da sie auch darin eine tierquälerische Komponente sieht –, deuten ihr Verhalten und ihre Sprache auf eine Ideologie hin, die sich darauf beschränkt, einen Schuldigen für Tierquälerei zu identifizieren, ohne sich den Komplexitäten der Tierschutzproblematik zu stellen. Alena spricht von »species fascism« (S. 82), von einer faschistischen Behandlung der Tiere durch den Menschen. Sie zitiert den als Tierschützer bekannten jüdisch-amerikanischen Schriftsteller Isaac Bashevis Singer mit dem Satz »Everyday is Auschwitz for the animals« (S. 86). Und schließlich stellt sie Jim gegenüber fest, dass ›der Mensch‹ eine Seuche sei – »we are the plague« (S. 114). Solche verallgemeinernden Aussagen ignorieren, dass nicht alle Menschen für industriell organisierte Tierquälerei verantwortlich sind und davon profitieren, sondern vor allem Angehörige der sozialen Eliten und der Mittelschichten in den Industrieländern. Mit der pauschalen Verurteilung ›des‹ Menschen wird darüber hinaus die besondere Verantwortung ignoriert, die die Spezies Mensch aufgrund ihrer überlegenen intellektuellen und moralischen Fähigkeiten nun einmal hat, wenn es darum geht, eine moralisch verantwortungsvolle Lösung für Probleme des Tierschutzes zu finden. Alenas Rhetorik wie ihr Verhalten Jim gegenüber signalisieren somit auch Egoismus und Menschenverachtung. Menschenverachtung als konzeptionelle Grundlage für den Tierschutz wird in *Carnal Knowledge* als überaus fragwürdig dargestellt.

Der Widerspruch zwischen radikalem Tierschutz-Ideal und seiner konkreten Umsetzung zeigt sich am drastischsten im fatalen Ausgang der Truthahn-Befreiungsaktion. Ihr Scheitern entlarvt die angewandte Strategie als unüberlegten Aktionismus, der sein Ziel jämmerlich verfehlt. Eine letztlich negative Einschätzung der radikalen Tierschutzbewegung zeigt sich schließlich im Spiel mit Bedeutungsgehalten, die im Namen des Hundes Alf stecken. Alfs Name setzt sich aus den Anfangsbuchstaben des Namens der radikalen Tierschutzorganisation Animal Liberation Front (ALF) zusammen, Alena hatte dem Laborversuchstier bewusst diesen Namen gegeben. In ironischer Brechung drückt sich in ihm jedoch nicht etwa die Stärke dieser Bewegung, sondern ihr im Grunde desolater Zustand aus. Alfs Name suggeriert, dass sie in einem ebenso erbärmlichen Zustand ist wie der Hund aufgrund der als Versuchstier erfahrenen Misshandlungen. Aus der Sicht Jims lässt sich die Einschätzung der Bewegung entsprechend seiner ersten Begegnung mit Alf interpretieren: Er fühlt sich sowohl vom Hund als auch von der Bewegung ›angepinkelt‹, d. h. missbraucht und ausgenutzt.

»*After the Plague*«

Auch *After the Plague* ist im Bereich der Thematik Umwelt- und Naturschutz verankert. Boyle greift die von – gerade auch radikalen – Umweltschützern oft geäußerte Warnung auf, dass der naturwissenschaftlich-technokratische Glaube an eine absolute Beherrschbarkeit der Kräfte der Natur irrig ist und im schlimmsten Fall zur Auslöschung der menschlichen Existenz führen kann. Im vorliegenden Szenario verursacht eine Mutation des Ebola-Virus binnen kürzester Zeit eine weltweite Seuche, die mit den Mitteln der Medizin nicht bekämpft werden kann und der deshalb nur wenige entkommen. Boyles Ich-Erzähler Francis Halloran III. – kurz Jed genannt – gehört zu einer Handvoll Überlebender in den USA, die sich plötzlich in einer fast völlig entvölkerten Welt zurechtfinden müssen. In ironischer Brechung typischer Merkmale von Katastrophengeschichten, vor allem des Katastrophenfilms, erforscht Boyle im Bericht seines Erzählers mögliche Reaktionen auf den Untergang einer Zivilisation, deren soziale und ökonomische Infrastruktur quasi über Nacht aufgehört hat zu existieren und deren materielle Manifestationen wie Häuser, Geschäfte oder auch Autos plötzlich als Relikte einer untergegangenen Welt angesehen werden müssen.

Der Erzähler Jed informiert gleich im ersten Abschnitt über den Stand der Dinge nach Abklingen der Seuche, ehe er seine Geschichte im Anschluss rückblickend, den Gang der Ereignisse chronologisch nachvollziehend, erzählt. Zum Zeitpunkt des Ausbruchs der Seuche befindet er sich in einer abgeschieden gelegenen Hütte in den Bergen der Sierra Nevada im südlichen Kalifornien. Über das Radio erreichen ihn die bestürzenden Nachrichten. Während der folgenden Tage beginnt er das Ausmaß der Katastrophe zu erahnen, in Augenschein kann er es jedoch erst nehmen, als er mit Sarai, einer jungen Frau, die sich in den Bergen verirrt und dadurch ebenfalls überlebt hat, in die Ebene hinunterfährt. Er berichtet weiter über die folgenden Monate seines Lebens im fast menschenleeren Gebiet um Santa Barbara. Nach einem Streit zieht Sarai aus dem gemeinsam bezogenen Haus aus, kurze Zeit später trifft Jed jedoch Felicia, die er noch aus der Zeit vor Ausbruch der Seuche kennt, und beginnt mit ihr zusammenzuleben. Die Geschichte endet mit einer weiteren Begegnung: Am Strand treffen Jed und Felicia auf Howard, den verschollen und tot geglaubten Freund Sarais.

After the Plague parodiert in etlichen Merkmalen den typischen Aufbau populärkultureller Katastrophendarstellungen. Zunächst fehlt der Geschichte der Held, der angesichts der drohenden Katastrophe über sich hinauswächst und trotz schmerzhafter persönlicher Verluste wesentlich zur Überwindung der Krise beitragen kann. Der Erzähler Jed hält sich ganz im Gegenteil fern vom grausigen Geschehen und ist auf Selbstschutz bedacht. Zudem arbeitet Boyle bei der Handlungsführung mit Mitteln der Komödie und nicht etwa – den drastischen Ereignissen eher entsprechend – mit solchen der Tragödie: Nach einigen Irrungen und Wirrungen finden zwei Paare, Jed und Felicia sowie Sarai und Howard, relativ wohlbehalten zueinander und signalisieren damit den Fortbestand der menschlichen Zivilisation. Schließlich verblüffen Stil, Ton und auch einige Aussagen des Erzählers Jed, die unerwartet keinen anhaltenden Schock, Traumatisierung, Trauer oder Klagen zum Ausdruck bringen, sondern deutlich werden lassen, dass er sich offenbar binnen weniger Monate recht gut mit der neuen Realität arrangieren konnte. Zwar äußert er Bedauern und Bestürzung, zwar beschreibt er Phasen der Angst, doch drücken gleich die ersten Sätze der Geschichte ein recht hohes Maß an Gelassenheit und sogar Zufriedenheit aus. In ihnen stellt Jed nicht nur fest, dass das Leben nach der Seuche »anders«, sondern auch »more relaxed and expansive, more natural« (S. 119) geworden sei. Zusammengenommen zeigen all diese Gestaltungsmerkmale, dass es sich hier um einen Erzähler handelt, dem die amerikanische Zivilisation, so wie er sie kannte –

und als Sozialwissenschaftler hatte er sich mit ihr gründlich beschäftigt –, nicht wirklich bewahrenswert gewesen zu sein scheint.

Allerdings deutet sich in der Geschichte auch an, dass die nun neu aufzubauende Zivilisation von keinem neuen Typ von Menschen getragen sein dürfte. Vor wie nach der Katastrophe ist das Zusammenleben der Menschen nämlich weitgehend von Isolation und einem gehörigen Aggressionspotenzial gekennzeichnet. Wer erwartet hat, dass die gemeinsam überlebte Seuche in den Überlebenden Gefühle der Sympathie oder Empathie geweckt hat, die zu solidarischem Handeln motivieren, sieht sich getäuscht. Das Verhältnis von Jed und Sarai ist von Aggression und Hass geprägt, die wenigen Überlebenden, die im verlassenen Stadtgebiet auftauchen, scheuen den Kontakt zueinander – teilweise sicher noch immer aus Angst vor Ansteckung, teilweise jedoch wohl auch, da sich Verhaltensmuster fortsetzen, die die Zeit vor der Seuche geprägt haben und die auf die starke Individualisierung oder gar Atomisierung der amerikanischen Gesellschaft verweisen. Von Bedeutung ist hierbei, dass die Seuche eine Radikalisierung selbstgewählter Formen der Isolation bewirkt – und diese damit quasi ad absurdum führt: Sämtliche Hauptfiguren hatten sich aus ihrem Alltag zurückgezogen. Der Wissenschaftler Jed nimmt ein Forschungssemester und fährt in eine einsam gelegene Hütte in den Bergen, um dort einen autobiographischen Roman zu schreiben; Felicia testet einen »sensory deprivation tank«, einen von John C. Lilly in den 1950er-Jahren entwickelten Isolationstank, in dessen Innern Menschen, im Dunkeln und in warmem Salzwasser liegend, über viele Stunden lang völlig abgeschottet von der Außenwelt Entspannung und Selbsterkenntnis finden sollten; Sarai und Howard schließlich wollen sich fernab von jeglicher Zivilisation in der amerikanischen Wildnis regenerieren.

Letztere Aktion kann darüber hinaus als satirischer Seitenhieb auf die Wildnisbegeisterung gelesen werden, die weite Teile der amerikanischen Umwelt- und Naturschutzbewegung seit ihrer Entstehungszeit im 19. Jahrhundert kennzeichnet und die auch die amerikanische Umweltpolitik auf Kosten der Beschäftigung mit sozialen Problemen des Umweltschutzes in Großstädten, etwa der Umweltverschmutzung, lange dominiert hat. Die Wildnisliebhaber Sarai und Howard werden eingeführt als Wanderer, die sich, was Ausrüstung und Versorgung angeht, mit dem größtmöglichen Komfort in die unzivilisierte Wildnis begeben. Die neueste High-Tech-Bekleidung etwa, oder auch die Delikatessen, die zunächst ihre Mahlzeiten darstellen, sind exklusive Produkte eben jener Zivilisation, der entflohen werden soll, und konterkarieren den Wunsch nach einem einfachen Leben in der Natur. Regeneration in der Wildnis erweist sich als eine Erfahrung, die man sich leisten können muss. Auch wenn der Urlaub für die beiden zur Rettung wird, auch wenn somit die Wildnis tatsächlich eine ›Neugeburt‹ in eine dramatisch veränderte Realität ermöglicht, wird sie doch auch zum Alptraum. Sarai überlebt ohne Nahrung und Unterkunft nur dadurch, dass sie Jeds Hütte findet. Schließlich deutet die gesamte Geschichte an, dass sich nach der Seuchenkatastrophe der Begriff von Wildnis dramatisch verändern dürfte. Während vorher unter Wildnis ausgewiesene Naturschutzgebiete, etwa Nationalparks, zu verstehen sind, die im Grunde gar keine ›wilde‹ Natur mehr enthalten, da sie vom Menschen verwaltet und gepflegt werden, ist nun, da die menschliche Kontrolle der Natur zusammengebrochen ist, zunehmend der gesamte Lebensraum der verbliebenen Menschheit als Wildnis zu verstehen. Zeichen dafür, dass sich die Natur Lebensraum zurückerobert, gibt es viele: die Murmeltiere, die Koyoten und der Bär, die nach dem Verschwinden der menschlichen Bevölkerung den 28-Seelen-Ort Fish Fry Flats in Besitz nehmen, sowie die allenthalben wuchernde Vegetation markieren das Einsetzen dieses Prozesses.

»Peep Hall«

In *Peep Hall* konfrontiert Boyle seine Leserschaft ein weiteres Mal mit einem Ich-Erzähler, dessen festgefügte Alltagsroutine plötzlich aus den Angeln gehoben wird. Hart Simpson, von Beruf Barkeeper und ansonsten ein Mensch, der zurückgezogen lebt und sehr auf Distanz zu anderen Menschen bedacht ist, erfährt von der Existenz eines Unternehmens in seiner allernächsten Nachbarschaft, das die meisten seiner Nachbarn zu einer Protestaktion veranlasst. Nur wenige Häuser entfernt, mitten im respektablen Mittelklasse-Vorort, steht Peep Hall, ein nur von jungen Frauen bewohntes, als College-Wohnheim eingerichtetes Haus, in dem in allen Räumen Webcams installiert sind, die einer zahlenden Internet-Kundschaft rund um die Uhr Live-Bilder von den Aktivitäten der Bewohnerinnen zur Verfügung stellen. Ausgerechnet bei ihm, der unerwartete Kontakte hasst, taucht eines Nachmittags eine der Pseudo-Studentinnen, Samantha, auf. Sie bittet ihn, sich der Unterschriftenaktion der empörten Nachbarn gegen das Etablissement zu verweigern. Fasziniert von Sam, abonniert Hart umgehend die Internet-Seite, verbringt die folgenden Tage viele Stunden vor dem Monitor und vernachlässigt dabei sowohl seine Arbeit als auch seine sonstigen, den Tag strukturierenden Aktivitäten. Im Kontakt mit einer Frau, die sich eher exhibitionistisch verhält, ist aus dem so sehr auf die Unversehrtheit seiner Privatsphäre bedachten Hart ein Mann geworden, der anonym in die Privatsphäre anderer eindringt. Aus der voyeuristischen Aktivität wird dann jedoch eine konkret sichtbare. Hart hat einen Beschützerinstinkt für Sam entwickelt und macht sich darum auf den Weg zu Peep Hall, um sie und die anderen jungen Frauen vor dem Protest und der drohenden Vertreibung zu warnen.

Zentrale Gegenstände der Geschichte sind somit die Phänomene des Voyeurismus und des Exhibitionismus, die in weiten Teilen einer von der protestantischen Arbeitsethik geprägten amerikanischen Gesellschaft tabuisiert sind bzw.

als unmoralisch verurteilt werden. Boyle lotet somit eine weitere Facette der amerikanischen Mittelklasse-Existenz aus. Gleichzeitig wirft die Geschichte aber auch die Frage nach den psychischen Beweggründen auf, die diesen Phänomenen zugrunde liegen mögen. In der Gestaltung vor allem des Erzählers Hart zeigt sich dabei in besonderem Maße Boyles Weigerung, in seinen Texten deutliche moralisch wertende Signale zu setzen. Moralische Bewertung bleibt Sache seines Lesers oder seiner Leserin, und auch für diese stellt sich die Aufgabe bei genauerer Lektüre als nicht ganz so einfach heraus – vor allem weil das Handeln und Verhalten des Protagonisten eine unterschwellig komische bzw. tragikomische Qualität aufweisen.

Die Gestaltung der Figur des Hart Simpson lässt ein Persönlichkeitsbild entstehen, das neurotische Züge zeigt. Sein zwanghaft anmutendes Beharren auf einer ungestörten Privatsphäre und das Bedürfnis nach absoluter Kontrolle seines Tages- und Wochenablaufs, die vor allem dem Zweck dienen, nicht überraschend mit anderen Menschen konfrontiert zu werden, können als soziale Phobie, als Angst vor Menschen, gedeutet werden. Hinzu kommen Harts ebenfalls zwanghaft anmutende Versuche, sowohl einen Roman als auch eine Master-Arbeit zu schreiben, die beide ein latentes Gefühl der Angst und der Bedrohung ansprechen. Hart versucht seit geraumer Zeit eine Romanhandlung zu entwickeln, die von der Erfahrung der Vereinsamung einer alten Frau ihren Ausgang nehmen soll. Es handelt sich um Grandma Rivers, die von ihrer Großfamilie, von Kindern, Enkeln und Urenkeln, vergessen wird, in einem primitiven Wohncontainer in einem Trailerpark leben muss und schließlich auch noch von einem tollwütigen Fuchs angefallen wird. Seine Master-Arbeit versucht Hart seit nunmehr über elf Jahren zu schreiben, und zwar zum Thema der Klaustrophobie in Franz Kafkas fiktionalen Texten. Beide Projekte deuten an, dass Hart die Auseinandersetzung mit für ihn existenziell wichtigen Themen indirekt, aus einer Sicherheit bietenden intellektuellen Distanz heraus sucht: mit dem distanzierten Blick des Autors, der eine fiktionale Welt erfindet, und mit dem distanzierten Blick des Wissenschaftlers, der sein von ihm, dem Subjekt, deutlich unterschiedenes Objekt analysiert.

Eine tragikomische Qualität erhält die Zeichnung der Figur dadurch, dass Hart mit so vielen seiner Vorsätze und Projekte scheitert und dass vor allem das Ausgangsszenario seines Romanprojekts geradezu absurde Züge aufweist. Mit seinen beiden Buchprojekten kommt er nicht voran und sein Bemühen, sich vor äußeren Eindringlingen zu schützen, scheitert spätestens an Sams Auftauchen. Komisch wirkt oft der Stil, in dem Hart die Geschehnisse zusammenfasst. Ohne es zu merken, offenbart er in der Schilderung der Ereignisse immer wieder eine gewisse Naivität, etwa als seine Füße beim ersten Auftauchen Sams sein Versteck auf der Veranda preisgeben. Die Wiedergabe seiner überaus detaillierten Beobachtungen – von Orten und Menschen der äußeren wie der digital zur Verfügung stehenden Realität – und vor allem die Passagen, in denen er, von einem schlechten Gewissen geplagt, über seinen Status als Voyeur nachdenkt, erhalten dann schließlich eine gleichzeitig schockierende wie entwaffnend-komische Qualität. Hart ist sich durchaus bewusst, mit welchen unschmeichelhaften Attributen z. B. seine Nachbarn seine Surf-Aktivitäten belegen würden, gleichzeitig ist er jedoch süchtig geworden nach der Beobachtung der Frauen in Peep Hall. Die Ambivalenz der Figur Hart äußert sich schließlich darin, dass zumindest ein Teil der Faszination dieses Voyeurs darin gründet, dass er nicht einfach seine sexuellen, anders nicht lebbaren Bedürfnisse befriedigen möchte, sondern Sam gegenüber einen Beschützerinstinkt entwickelt – ein Gefühl, das psychologisch durchaus als Projektion interpretiert werden kann.

Sylvia Mayer

Inhalt

Englische Fremdsprachentexte

IN RECLAMS UNIVERSAL-BIBLIOTHEK

Crime and Horror

American Crime Stories: John Collier, Stanley Ellin, John D. MacDonald, James M. Cain, Henry Slesar, Margaret Millar. 167 S. UB 9268

Robert Bloch: Psycho. 239 S. UB 9066

Raymond Chandler: Killer in the Rain. 128 S. UB 9198 – The Big Sleep. 377 S. UB 9009

Arthur Conan Doyle: The Speckled Band. Four Sherlock Holmes Stories. 160 S. UB 9003

Daphne du Maurier: The Birds. 76 S. UB 9287 – Don't Look Now (Wenn die Gondeln Trauer tragen). 109 S. UB 9054

English Crime Stories: Margery Allingham, Anthony Berkeley, P. D. James, Dick Francis, Dorothy Sayers. 165 S. UB 9254

Graham Greene: The Third Man. 173 S. UB 9180

Patricia Highsmith: A Shot from Nowhere. Six Stories. 160 S. UB 9262 – The Talented Mr. Ripley. 437 S. UB 9145

Horror Stories of the Twentieth Century: Algernon Blackwood, Muriel Spark, Noel Langley, Patricia Highsmith, Stephen King. 151 S. UB 9255

John Le Carré: Call for the Dead. 240 S. UB 9048

Edgar Allan Poe: The Murders in the Rue Morgue. 80 S. UB 9088

Robert Louis Stevenson: The Strange Case of Dr. Jekyll and Mr. Hyde. 119 S. UB 9167

Philipp Reclam jun. Stuttgart